LIVING IN 22ND CENTURY

New-Way Governance

By Viswa

Credits

Cover Images: Dr. Ananya
Motivation: Bhavishya
Support: My best-half and beloved Vani
Best wishes: Near and Dear

Dedicated to my family and friends, without whose support, inspiration, motivation, encouragement, and best wishes this work would not have been possible.

Copyrights

First edition First published by QCLOUD 2025
ISBN: 979-8-9995493-2-7
Cover art by Dr. Ananya

Contents

The Prelude

The year was 2101 AD. Humanity teetered at the crossroads of its own making.

In a quiet valley, *Vish* lay on a simple bed, his eyes closed, yet his mind wide awake. Through his racing thoughts, he perceived the world's turmoil—torn between the weight of old, destructive habits and the rising glow of new possibilities, a clear unrest of gigantic proportions. The choices were: embrace transformation or face further degeneration.

"We owe this to ourselves," his thoughts displayed on the holoscreen to the folks watching intently, reverberating through the room and out to the world audience. "We owe this to our survival."

His thoughts flooded like a gushing torrent of data streams. Humanity had confronted an obvious choice: either hold on to destructive habits, turning dear Earth into a wasteland, or tap into the progressive human spirit to realize a thriving planet.

The choice was clear—follow the progressive human spirit. This path would foster prosperous earthly living and enable humanity's expansion as an interplanetary species.

Vish had developed the *New-Way Living* ideology over decades of observation and contemplation. Throughout history some of these ideas have been tried in various forms, but not all yielded meaningful relevance or tangible positive results. He recognized the urgent need for bold, practical solutions to help humanity thrive. These solutions had to be both functional and sustainable, addressing people's needs and desires across all areas of life—physical, social, and spiritual.

Vish considered *Abraham Maslow*'s Hierarchy of Needs from the early 20th century and reclassified these needs and wants to support 22nd century times. This evolved classification of needs supported *CHEFS* (Clothing, Health, Education, Food and Security) and *LifeScore* concepts that glue together New-Way Governance ideologies.

Vish canonically recognized human needs as falling into five essential categories:

Sustenance needs:

Basic—food, health, clothing, education, shelter, and safety.

Social needs:

Belonging—a sense of belonging and acceptance.

Esteem—freedom, security, dignity, and respect.

Spiritual needs:

Self-actualization—realizing self and reflections.

Nirvana—transcend from personal to impersonal.

Vish added the qualities of Reflection—a conscious pause and evaluation, and Nirvana—a peaceful state of existence—to the Needs.

His gaze upon the New-Way world of the 22nd century filled him with profound hope as communities, innovators, leaders, and common citizens awakened to humanity's true purpose and potential.

The New-Way tenets declared that actions diminishing human well-being and survival were the gravest crimes against humanity. This new kind of existence did not require abandoning individual ambitions. Instead, it sought to remove constraints on human potential. Actions of greed, coercion, deception, and harm were recognized as the negative primitive forces that had trapped humanity in downward spiral and in cyclical struggles throughout history.

This was the hope Vish had labored relentlessly to bring forth. He was filled with quiet joy as he saw that realization began to take root in the early 22nd century in the hearts and minds of the population around the world. However, deep-seated resistance persisted from dogmatists and oligarchs, who benefited and thrived from the old order. They would not yield to change even if that was for the greater good. Ahead lay trials and tribulations marked by violence, subversion, and inevitable setbacks in the battles for change. This was the clarion call to all who heard Vish's words. They owed it to their descendants, whose unborn faces should motivate their most honest and valiant efforts.

His most resolute followers—Maria, Adit, Lea, Kirl, Grace, Sparq—known as *Core Influencers*, and many others spread the vital New-Way message across cultures, nations, and continents. They helped catalyze a new era of human civilization founded on precepts not of conflict, oppression, selfishness, and destruction, but of cooperation, freedom, collectivism, and construction. *In this era of new way governance, people were judged by their positive impact on society.* This shift in perspective redefined leadership and success, emphasizing stewardship, sustainability, and social responsibility.

Vish was very proud of the New-Way followers who worked hard for a society where individuals had freedom, respect, dignity, and equal chances to take part. The Core influencers had taken his ideas and adapted them to unique cultural contexts and challenges in real-world implementations. Together, they were helping dawn a new human civilization that celebrated diversity while uniting around common values of compassion, justice, and sustainability.

As Vish reflected on their achievements, he knew the journey had just begun. The forces of the old world, with vested interests and entrenched power structures, would not relinquish their hold easily. There would be battles ahead, both ideological and physical. But Vish also knew that momentum was on their side. The awakening was spreading, and with each new adherent, the New-Way movement grew stronger.

He thought of the countless individuals worldwide who had embraced New-Way thinking. From scientists and artists to farmers and activists, people from all walks of life came together to build a better future. They formed networks of cooperation, sharing knowledge and resources, supporting each other in their endeavors, all in the open. This grassroots movement—fundamental participatory action—was the true power behind the change.

The Burden of Injustice

Vish had defined "Primal Constructs" with regards to the New-Way Governance as "*the core organizing mechanisms to build our benign behaviors that influence actions and decisions in social contexts.*" These organizing mechanisms were justice, economics, politics, and society, all tied together by spirituality.

For centuries, societies had ignored stark social inequalities. Economic, political, and social structures had caused lopsided growth in pursuit of progress using its very narrow definition. These primal constructs had missed the all-important non-material aspect of living: *Spirituality.* Politics, economy, and society without spirituality chased self-centered aspects of human life. Prevalent selfish governance policies resulted in sustained inequalities of income, health, opportunities, voices, and rights.

Vish was seen lamenting what the primal constructs had become and deteriorated into selfish tools by the end of the 21st century.

Economic systems have produced numerous socio-economic failures. In capitalism businesses prioritized profits over fair wages and working conditions, exploiting workers on a massive scale. Growth obsession drove rampant resource depletion and pollution. Consumerism created unsustainable materialism and waste, with fast fashion brands producing disposable clothing destined for landfills. Alternatively, hybrid economic models yielded stagnant growth, widespread famine, and authoritarian regimes. These and many other 21st century economic maladies highlighted the downsides of unregulated capitalism, oppressive communist regimes, and stifling socialist ideas, prompting calls for reforms or alternative systems.

Political systems were plagued by concentrations of power, money, and emotional manipulation. Extreme polarization between political groups stalled progress and fostered hostility, with legislative gridlock over critical issues like healthcare reforms and budget approvals. The concentration of power in individual leaders or select groups eroded democratic processes and freedoms. This erosion was evidenced by restrictive laws on press freedom and suppression of dissent in authoritarian regimes. Such an encroachment on freedom was seen even in modern democracies. Leaders manipulated public emotions through oversimplified solutions and divisive rhetoric, scapegoating immigrants and minorities for economic problems to gain support from vulnerable populations. Corrupt politicians and governments routinely distort facts to mislead the public and keep power, spreading misinformation and disinformation to discredit rising voices and opposition parties.

Social systems perpetuated deliberate inequalities through divisive methods rooted in religion, selfishness, and exploitation. Individual success was prioritized over community well-being, creating hierarchies that marginalized vulnerable groups. Gender roles restricted women's leadership opportunities, while profit-driven healthcare denied access to those who couldn't afford treatment. These societal issues illustrate how existing social constructs limited progress, deepened inequality, and stifled diversity.

Spirituality, while offering the promise of deep personal exploration that can lead to greater self-awareness, inner peace, and connection with the world, was often discredited, corrupted and exploited. While spirituality stood apart from organized religion, it was often appropriated by religious institutions and manipulated to justify unethical conduct and self-serving agendas. Spiritual beliefs were weaponized to justify abuse, with perpetrators misappropriating religious texts to excuse physical, emotional, psychological, or sexual abuse, claiming divine authority or duty. "Spiritual bypassing" allowed people to ignore pressing real-world problems. Manipulative leaders used spiritual rhetoric to justify inaction on social and environmental crises, claiming that suffering was divinely ordained or was necessary for growth.

Below, we shall dwell on degradation of each of these pillars of the primal constructs—economics, politics, society and spirituality using examples that highlight their current shortcomings.

Let us shine a spotlight on the outcomes of prevailing Economic policies through a few of the key illustrative examples:

Exploitation of Labor: Businesses prioritize profits over fair wages and working conditions, leading to worker exploitation. Sweatshops in many countries with low wages, long hours, and unsafe conditions.

Environmental Degradation: Focus on narrow definition of growth leads to overuse and wastage of natural resources and environmental harm. Large-scale deforestation in the Amazon driven by agricultural and industrial expansion.

Consumerism: Encourages unsustainable consumption and materialism, creating waste and dissatisfaction.

Fast fashion brands produce cheap, disposable clothing that ends up in landfills.

These and other such economic issues highlight the downsides of unregulated capitalism, oppressive communist regimes, stifling socialist ideas, often prompting calls for reforms or alternative systems.

Now consider Political systems. These were plagued by power, money and selfishness. Here are a few key outcomes:

Partisanship and Polarization: Extreme division between political groups stalls progress and fosters hostility. legislative gridlock over issues like healthcare reform or budget approvals.

Authoritarianism: Concentration of power in one leader or select group that erodes freedoms and democratic processes. Restrictive laws on press and dissent in autocratic regimes.

Populism and Demagoguery: Leaders manipulate public emotions with oversimplified solutions and divisive rhetoric. Politicians blaming immigrants for economic issues to gain support from susceptible citizens.

Ideologies rooting for human well-being were ridiculed and replaced by selfish principles. Ethics and morals were abandoned in everyday practice. These systemic flaws erode the legitimacy of public institutions, leading to diminished civic engagement, increased polarization, and worsening social inequalities.

Let us glance at the Societies at large. The social fabric was riddled with inequalities. Social norms were deliberately designed to forge divisions. These subversions were ably enabled by religion, selfishness, exploitation and lack of compassion. Here are a few of the key outcomes:

Social Alienation: The focus on individual success undermines community and social well-being through idolization and hero worship.

Reinforcement of Inequality: Unethical social constructs often create and perpetuate hierarchies that marginalize certain groups. Gender roles limit women's opportunities in leadership positions.

Healthcare Inequities: Healthcare often becomes a profit-driven industry, limiting access for those who cannot afford it. Inflated cost of life-saving insulin, making it unaffordable for diabetics.

These societal issues illustrate the existing social constructs that limit progress, deepen inequality, and stifle diversity.

Finally, let us look at Spirituality which is a deep personal exploration that can lead to greater self-awareness, inner peace, and connection with the world around us. While spirituality is distinct from religion, religious practices embrace it only by abusing it and incorrectly applying it to unethical practices for selfish gains. Here are a few of such misapplications:

Spiritual Manipulation and Control: Using spiritual beliefs to justify abuse—An abuser citing religious texts or beliefs to excuse physical, emotional, psychological, or sexual abuse, claiming it's their right or duty.

Spiritual Bypassing: Ignoring real-world problems - A person using spiritual beliefs to justify inaction on social or environmental issues, claiming that everything is part of a divine plan or that suffering is necessary for spiritual growth.

Harmful Spiritual Practices: Denial of medical care - A person might be discouraged or prevented from seeking necessary medical treatment, relying solely on spiritual healing methods.

True spirituality fosters love, compassion, and respect. Instead, humanity witnessed exploitation of gullible people in the name of spiritual practice, with leaders promoting harm, control, or isolation. Indeed, humanity had come a long way from cave dwelling to modern living at the end of the 21st century. But the progress was sparse and lopsided. Only a minority devoured the benefits while the vast majority were left behind, clamoring for the fruits of progress.

The burden of inequality adversely affected the sustainability and endangered preservation of the human species. The misuse of primal constructs resulted in inching toward the extinction of the human species.

The LifeScore Metric

Vish believed that life's "larger context" lay in humanity's need to collectively survive with equitable well-being. His New-Way Ideology was based on this larger context, defined as an intertwined set of modern principles—judicial, political, economic, social, and spiritual constructs.

Vish believed that "Human Life is Simple and is defined by the sum of its actions and consequences," expanding on *John Galsworthy*'s 1867 assertion that "A man is the sum of his actions." This belief became a tool and life method, functioning as an *ubuntu* or *dharma* for human well-being.

Drawing upon the knowledge of human history and the wisdom of its lessons, Vish reasoned that sustainable well-being could indeed be achieved equitably in this generation—and endure into futurity.

He defined Human Life as "*Sum of Actions for Self and Selfless*," condensing and formalizing that notion into a below mathematical formula applicable in real life:

$$\sum_{i=1}^{n} (\text{Self} \pm X_i) + \sum_{j=1}^{n} (\text{Selfless} \times (\pm Y_j))$$

LifeScore = Actions [Σ (forSelf ± X) $_{1\cdots n}$ + Σ (forSelfless × ±Y) $_{1\cdots n}$]

forSelf → actions that benefit self (Context)

forSelfless → actions that benefit others (Context)

X, Y → numerical weights assigned by society/culture

± Operator → helping actions as positive, harming as negative

× Operator → order of magnitude, used for selfless actions

For higher impact, use a higher context number

LifeScore's weights and qualifiers reflected cultural contexts, blending universal humanistic values with local cultural considerations. The formula was evidently weighted toward altruistic actions, thereby institutionalizing and strengthening the role of spirituality. Community/context weightage examples:

- Lesser ability person receives Child-level weightage
- Criminal actions receive negative weightage
- Selfish actions receive less weightage
- Selfless actions receive higher weightage

In New-Way Governance, Vish introduced this novel action/consequence scoring system—the *LifeScore*—which became a central tenet of the governance. Governments employed the LifeScore metric to administer individual-level rewards or deterrents. LifeScore entitled people to material comforts according to their individual score, the only way to earn material comforts beyond subsistence entitlements.

This notion appeared simplistic and utopian, yet the Core Team remained convinced of its feasibility in New-Way Governance. The Core Team masterfully used a *triumvirate of advanced technologies*—Artificial Super Intelligence (ASI), Quantum Information Processing (QIP), and Nuclear Fusion energy (NFE), available in the early 22nd century to implement LifeScore and provided detailed instructions for New-Way Governance.

LifeScore values hinged on two fundamental measures: one, the *intent* behind each action—selfish or selfless, second, its *impact*—beneficial or harmful. Accumulated over the course of an individual's life, these scores constituted a personal reserve that could be exchanged for material benefits and privileges. LifeScore, as a dynamic metric, would decrease when used for material benefits but could be replenished through continued positive contributions by one's actions. LifeScore accounting was securely managed using Blockchain technologies, with checks and balances as established by communities. The metric was updated using combination of autonomous and active feedback from the community, made possible by 22nd century technological advancements. By using the LifeScore formula as an objective metric, communities could accurately derive rewards and/or penalties for their members.

Vish maintained that *all human actions and inactions carry consequences; they either help or harm.* Whether something was judged as good or bad, useful or useless, depended entirely on humanistic social contexts and collective perspectives. This principle of *Material and Spiritual Consequentialism* became the cornerstone of New-Way Ideology, guiding its application across justice, economics, politics, and society.

Vish offered a profound definition of life as *a serendipitous occurrence composed of distinct parts that, together, formed a unified whole greater than the sum of its parts.* This life was a complex blend of materials exhibiting unique characteristics, setting it apart from its individual components. It embodied both individual and collective consciousness simultaneously.

He articulated that within a cause-and-effect paradigm, human actions serve as causes and the outcomes as effects. In his view, there was no inherent or hidden meaning to human existence beyond the consequences of one's actions. Therefore, one should act deliberately to create meaningful consequences. Furthermore, Vish reasoned that if destiny or inherent meaning existed in life, extinction events proved otherwise. When life began anew after such events, it restarted from scratch, retracing

Charles Darwin's evolutionary path once again—just like everything else in the universe.

Vish asked, "Since humans have the ability to create and destroy, why not channel these capacities positively—to construct, progress, and preserve? To be positive requires bravery and kindness."

Thus, Vish's motto: "*Be Creative. Be Positive. Be Kind.*"

Vish and Core Team

Mr. Vish, the absent protagonist, was from Nepal. He authored the seminal book *Life's Larger Context*, hereinafter referred to as *the Book*. We explore his teachings and philosophies through the actions and implementations of the Core Team, who, in turn, follow his Book. Vish believed that human life was as normal as having a chance beginning with a definitive ending but as special as leaving a consequential impact on its existence and perpetuation in the universe.

This was the early years of the 22nd century. The influencer actors propagated New-Way Ideology across the globe. Known as the Core Team, they were constituted by the global convention of New-Way Ideology adherents. It was composed of exemplary individuals selected on an as-needed basis.

The current Core Team consisted of Adit, Maria, Lea, and Kirl. These members implemented New-Way Ideology in select countries. The first wave of New-Way countries included Namibia, New Zealand, Slovenia, Sri Lanka, UAE, and Uruguay. The Core Team chose these countries because they were already relatively progressive, forward-looking, and small on their respective continents. Grace and Sparq led the New-Way *CHEFS* program.

The Core Team and CHEFS implementers of New-Way Ideology were:

Ms. Maria, a political scientist and fierce advocate for social justice, had worked tirelessly to improve administration and politics in countries worldwide. Her efforts in Uruguay created a New-Way model of governance now being replicated globally.

Mr. Adit, an economist and technologist, had been instrumental in developing sustainable economic models and technologies that balanced human well-being with a sustainable environment. His work led to innovations revolutionizing economics and transportation technologies globally.

Ms. Lea, a sociologist and environmentalist, had devised a New-Way social mechanism for peace and harmony. Her initiatives not only saved endangered species but also inspired a global movement toward biodiversity with human co-existence.

Mr. Kirl, a mathematician and spiritualist, used his skills to mediate conflicts and foster international cooperation. His efforts paved the way for New-Way alliances and a stronger global community.

Ms. Sparq, an educationalist and visionary leader from the UAE, championed the global implementation of learning and healthcare through sustenance CHEFS. She funded institutions of learning across Middle Eastern countries, sowing the seeds for knowledge-based economies.

Ms. Grace, a bio-scientist and humanitarian from Namibia, focused on empowering marginalized communities, ensuring they had a voice in shaping their futures. Her work brought hope and dignity to countless lives by implementing Food and Housing security using the CHEFS program.

These influencers, inspired by Vish's vision, took his ideas and adapted them to fit unique local and global contexts and challenges as relevant in the early 22nd century. Together, they were building a new social paradigm that celebrated diversity while uniting around common values of compassion, dignity, and justice.

Come, in the next few chapters let us trace the steps of these stalwarts through the brave new world of New-Way Living!

***

The Core

New-Way Core Team

We will shadow the Core influencers and highlight their journey as they implement the New-Way Ideology across the globe.

Adit

Adit was a fifty-year-old Japanese man from Kyoto, Japan. Short, sturdy, and reserved, his demeanor revealed him as a man of vast knowledge. He smiled often, and his patience added to his charm. He lived in Calgary while in Canada.

Today, Adit had a meeting scheduled with Folapr, a New-Way operative, at the log house near Flathead Lake in northern Montana. Flathead Lake receives its pristine waters from the Flathead and Swan rivers throughout the year. Adit was flying his personal custom-built intermodal transporter, the *Tresporter*. The mountainous landscape was stunning, offering a broad and beautiful view while flying over a thousand feet above the obstacles. He was flying from Calgary, Canada to Bigfork in Montana, USA—about two hundred nautical miles.

After about two hours, he neared his destination. A few minutes before landing, Adit skimmed through holographic private messages using his special glasses. These glasses, provided by the Core group, were linked to the wearer's DNA signature for deciphering holographic messages, making them highly secure and unusable by anyone else. An alternative way to read secure messages was to use eye contact-lenses genetically linked to the person. Adit hovered and touched down on a small flat rectangular thirty square feet area nestled in the thick forest. Mr. Folapr was already there, waiting for him. This meeting aimed to iron out a few specifics of Integrative Transportation technologies.

Adit flew an airplane like a contraption, a compact dual-seater and highly efficient personal transporter of his own design. Despite its small size, this vehicle could operate on land, in the air, and on water when transformed. The Tresporter while in motion could regenerate energy to sixty percent of the power used, whether on land, water, or in the air. He deployed various energy generation mechanisms such as solar-skin, windmill and kinetic energy conversions. Tresporter could be transformed into an airplane, a canoe, or a motorbike. Tresporter retained the two-seater configuration in all its transformations. The contraption used magnets from the Lanthanide series permanent magnets for magnetism instead of on/off electromagnets.

Folapr was tall and slender, standing almost six feet tall. Caucasian with a full head of hair—quite impressive for a fifty-year-old. Despite his thin frame, he appeared strong with well-defined, chiseled muscles. His personality was endearing. Folapr and Adit had known each other for several years now. Folapr had proven to be a reliable collaborator for the Core Team.

"How was the journey over the hilly terrain? Was it difficult due to the severe weather grounding flights in the area?" Folapr inquired.

"The flight was a bit bumpy due to turbulence and heavy rain in parts, but manageable," Adit responded. "The local small airports weren't suitable for my single engine land airplane today, so I opted for my Tresporter."

"Do you ever require a different vehicle for transportation?" Folapr asked with a smile.

"Yes, it doesn't fly to space!" Adit smiled back.

Folapr watched with amusement as Adit transformed his personal Tresporter into a motorbike. They rode the bike for about ten minutes to the nearby bank on Flathead Lake. Once there, Adit transformed the bike into a canoe. They planned to canoe from Bigfork to a westerly location on the Lakeside enroute to Polson. Folapr had a friend at Lakeside from whom they collected fishing gear, accessories, and food. They loaded the baggage and set off for Polson, fishing along the way in the tranquil, still waters, enjoying their time together.

On that beautiful summer afternoon around 2 pm, daylight was beginning to fade as mountain peaks and treetops obscured much of the sunlight. They could see fish even from a depth of about fifty feet in the clear waters. It was surreal to look deep into the river and follow the fish. Watching them swim and approach the bait was also a magical and trance-inducing experience. They both caught some fish from the clear, fresh river.

Adit caught Kokanee Salmon and Mountain Whitefish, while Folapr caught Rainbow Trout and Smallmouth Bass, local to this river. They released all the fish back into the waters. They tasted water from the river—it was excellent and felt revitalizing. They discussed diverse topics and happenings around the world with reference to New-Way Governance while enjoying the peace and privacy that fishing offered in that remote tranquil lake.

Upon reaching Polson, they disembarked on the shore. Adit then transformed the canoe back into the motorbike. They rode the bike a few miles into the Polson reservation to meet with Ksanka Herr, a mutual friend.

Folapr arranged the meeting with Ksanka to discuss details about Integrative Transportation. Ksanka, a Native American from Polson, shared his new communication methods that integrate with a few aspects of 22nd century transportation. Both Folapr and Ksanka were communication specialists trained in electronics and linguistics. Ksanka offered insights into groundbreaking inventions about energy conversion and storage. Adit was appreciative and receptive of these technologies, seeing how they provided independence to transportation.

Ksanka wirelessly transferred his notes to both Folapr and Adit's devices. The device called "CommBox" could be set up to securely accept wireless transfers remotely and globally. This device can be switched to become untraceable, even when it connects and transmits worldwide. It was always on and ready to exchange messages with the Core Team. After spending about an hour with Ksanka, Adit and Folapr biked back to the waters at Polson. Adit converted the bike back to canoe. They canoed back to Lakeside, returned the gear, and then headed back from shore to the log house at Bigfork on the yet again transformed bike.

They walked into a very unassuming log house that Folapr maintained in the area. It was a small dwelling of about three hundred square feet total, located about two miles from Bigfork town. This area was quite secluded, and few people were aware of this log house existence.

By 6 pm local time, they had both freshened up. Folapr, being a skilled cook, prepared delicious dishes, both vegan and non-vegan. He made vegan food for Adit and non-vegan for himself. They paired their meal with red wine that Folapr saved for special guests. These fine wines were a gift to Folapr from Kirl when he visited Bigfork the previous year. Kirl had brought these wines from his trip to Nordic countries. The region was experiencing a boom in wineries due to climate change. Extended summers had prompted locals to adapt to winemaking, creating a thriving new industry.

"The variety of vehicles currently used for human transport—Jet Packs, Drones, Hover Boards, Cable Cars, Vacuum Tunnels, and Levitation Autos—are all fascinating. However, they all still have one common limitation: in-flight refueling," Adit remarked.

"Indeed, as you suggested, the ultimate goal seems to be achieving refueling in transit without interrupting the journey. You have patented several refueling-in-transit (rFIT) technologies," Folapr responded.

“Absolutely. Incorporating these and other complementary technologies into everyday transportation that people can use is a substantial challenge. These technologies are still under development," Adit concurred, envisioning how a gravity assisted vacuum-tunnel transit could eliminate the need for refueling.

It was time for the meeting of the Core.

Adit pulled out the CommBox, a small communication device to facilitate remote communications. Folapr, a licensed amateur radio operator, had helped to create the CommBox. This was designed with high computing abilities using Optical and Quantum chips and featured quantum-safe encryption, making its communications unhackable.

The meeting agenda covered a wide range of topics, including transportation, communication, social norms, governance, healthcare, education, and space colonies. The attendees included Adit, Maria, Lea, Kirl, Grace, Sparq, and several of their confidantes.

Maria

Maria was a forty-five-year-old mestiza from Central Mexico. She was returning from space after attending a symposium on "Space Colonies and New-Way Governance" sponsored by New-Way Namibia. Mr. Amzoni went to the Spaceport in outer Los Angeles to receive her. She disembarked from the space vehicle, went through the sanitization process, removed her outer suit, and emerged from the gate—a five-minute routine for 22nd century space travelers.

Amzoni and Maria hugged and kissed. Amzoni summoned a self-drive auto from the parking lot. They hopped in and directed it to their beach home about an hour south of the Spaceport. The self-drive auto cost ten NeWay Crypto coins. These vehicles traveled by hovering above rough terrain but rode on the surface when the path was smooth. This method made the vehicle move smoothly like a boat on still water.

"Maria, you don't look tired even after space travel," Amzoni observed.

Maria's eyes sparkled with humor. "But you look exhausted after a mere 1500-mile journey from Kansas City."

"I had to go around some disruptions along the way. Who said traveling was easy on Earth, even with Level 5 autonomous driving and autopilot flying?" Amzoni wondered.

"Space travel to Earth-moon Selene has become so easy—it's no harsher than 8000-mile flights among many Earth destinations," Maria said, referring to the ease of space travel in the early 22nd century.

“Throughout the journey, I witnessed stark disparities in economic and health conditions. I saw people living in persistent squalor and battling life-threatening diseases. Yet the administration simply blamed the victims, claiming they refused to help themselves," Amzoni replied, his voice heavy with pain. “Demonstrations and disruptions are erupting everywhere along the route."

"I know, I was joking. Inequality was ignored, and it was the reason behind these chaotic struggles," Maria continued, hopeful of America that would accept New-Way solutions.

On this trip, Maria visited two colonies—one on Selene, Earth's moon, and another on a near-Earth space colony named Schutzgebiet (meaning "protectorate" in German), commissioned and maintained by Namibia. In her meetings with various colony agencies, Maria stressed the need to move away from a prescriptive, top-down approach to participative, bottom-up governance and administration.

Maria served on the advisory boards of the governments that had embraced New-Way Governance. She was a recognized expert in governance policies at both micro and macro levels across various forms of governments and organizations. Her expertise had earned her global recognition among the public and political leaders alike.

She agreed with Vish's principles that emphasized separating administration from politics. U.S. President Woodrow Wilson in the early 20th century first proposed this dichotomy between politics and administration. The New-Way Governance adopted this model. This model separated governance into two spheres: internal administration for domestic affairs and external diplomacy for international relations. This system had eliminated the traditional partisan politics. The dichotomy allowed leaders to collaborate globally while administrators focused on domestic needs—two independent yet interconnected functions.

In New-Way Governance, international politics focused on diplomacy, international treaties, trade agreements, and conflict resolution. It also addressed global issues such as human rights, space policies, environmental concerns, including water and mineral resources—and global security.

Meanwhile, traditional national politics was replaced by internal administration. The internal administration handled domestic matters such as CHEFS program, research and development, infrastructure, and spiritual well-being programs such as NSCs. Its purpose was to reflect and serve the interests and needs of the country's citizens.

Maria and Amzoni, who was from Iran, were married initially under traditional Marriage Law for about ten years. However, they transitioned into a New-Way marital relationship known as HappyChoice.

Their paths first crossed at a near-Earth orbital station. Maria was presenting New-Way Governance and the rapid changes occurring in various countries on Earth. Amzoni, a last-minute addition to the symposium in place of an absent researcher, made several intriguing observations about transparency in space colony governance. Maria acknowledged the relevance of these ideas and their worthiness for inclusion in implementing New-Way Governance for space colonies. This led them to meet again soon after her presentation to discuss various aspects of fair and equitable governance.

After six months of continuous exchanges and meetings, they happily cohabited and later married. They soon recognized that traditional marriage as a cultural institution was becoming obsolete worldwide. Having married traditionally in Mexico, they annulled their marriage in favor of a New-Way marital relationship. This New-Way relationship was described as a happy choice, *HappyChoice* as coined by Vish in his book.

HappyChoice stood for a true choice: to be together in consonance or separated in dissonance.

The taxi ride to their home was smooth, traveling through a few opulent and many destitute areas. Amzoni gazing out the window observed the stark contrast between poor and rich neighborhoods. This was true across the USA he thought.

Maria closed her eyes and swirled with thoughts about the economic and political situations in the USA. The economy was stuttering with inflation, budget deficits, and alarming disparity in wealth. There was severe unrest in mid-western America—some termed this brewing situation as rebellion, others as anti-national and seditionary. The unrest had resulted in disruptions to everyday lives in the Midwest and was spreading rapidly across the vast country much like Arab Spring in early 21st century.

The political systems on Earth were largely the Nation-State style of 21st century governments. A handful of small countries followed and implemented Inter-State systems proposed by New-Way Governance theories. Maria believed that selfish Nation-State regimes needed to be re-drawn towards a more inclusive New-Way Inter-State political system. Vish proposed this Inter-State system in a chapter titled "Dawn of New Age Governance" and offered insights and guidance with high-level implementation guidelines.

According to Maria, the age of 20th century City-State or 21st century Nation-State political concepts urgently needed replacement. The fresh approach should be Inter-State politics. Local governance was managed by inward administration, which delegated authority to a combination of elected and appointed local officials, while outward governance between countries was assigned to respective elected and appointed national leaders. Local councils and communities choose administrators or representatives based on a mix of knowledge, accomplishments, virtues, skills, and LifeScores. The triumvirate of advanced technologies in the 22nd century enabled the widespread adoption of New-Way governance, empowering councils, communities, and individuals to coordinate seamlessly—across local and international levels in real time.

Maria thought about the New-Way movement's unique approach to polity and administration. In this model, ground-level *needs* determined autonomous budgetary allocation to developmental programs and related field-level tasks. The budgetary system was completely automated, incorporating a real-time feedback-loop mechanism that allowed citizens, communities, and councils to take active part instantaneously. In this model, citizen voters elected representatives for two main roles. The first role was that of leaders who stand for their countries internationally, making decisions that have global significance while keeping their country's interests in mind. The second role was that of administrators, who were specialists in specific areas and were elected or appointed to manage internal administration.

While in deep thoughts Maria fell asleep for about 10 minutes. Then she woke up abruptly as the automobile lurched through stop-and-go traffic caused by street disturbances. These instantaneous eruptions, a manifestation of civil unrest, had become common and were witnessed all over the country.

Maria's work implementing New-Way governance was guided by Vish's concept of *Human Obligations* defined as "Actions for self and for others." Amzoni recognized Maria's instrumental role in setting up fair governance and observed how New-Way countries such as Namibia, New Zealand, Slovenia, Sri Lanka, the UAE, and Uruguay had experienced profound political transformation through their adoption of Vish's integrated approach to economics, politics, social organization, and spirituality.

"The framework and principles established by Vish for Fair Governance have enabled much of my own work to be practically and equitably applied," Maria expressed.

"This is not the utopia of Thomas More from the 15th century but a very practical and implementable governance applicable to all cultures and peoples, wherever they live on the planet. This is the dawn of New-Way Living," Maria emphasized. She also pointed out that the new governance model was now immune to corruption and other evils that plagued nations and societies leading up to the 22nd century.

"Yes, but only in the smaller countries that have embraced New-Way Ideology for Fair Governance," Amzoni agreed, recognizing the beginnings of the movement.

After about an hour, the taxi dropped them with luggage at their home. They went straight in and refreshed themselves quickly.

It was almost time for meeting with the Core.

Maria and Amzoni walked into another room. They both pulled out the CommBox gadgets for the meeting and wore the glasses used by Core Team members and their closest confidantes.

Lea

Lea, a forty-two-year-old athletic woman, was from France, originally from Chamonix, a small town near the Swiss border, but had moved to Paris where she spent most of her time. From her personal research experience in archaeology, anthropology, and sociology, Lea knew these areas profoundly influenced how societies peacefully live their lives yet co-exist amidst change, conflict, and chaos. She had accounted for almost every detail of life actions, whether chaotic or blissful, among societies on Earth and beyond in space.

Lea had studied major religions and belief systems from across the continents. She hypothesized that any belief system, whether with an omnipotent God or not (nontheistic), was in fact some form of religion. So, she didn't care much about discussions centered on religions. In line with Vish's teachings, Lea believed that belief systems must evolve and self-correct when they no longer benefit humanity, always considering the broader context of human well-being.

Lea was returning from a twenty-mile mountain bike ride. It's along a single-track balcony trail in the dramatic vertical landscape of Switzerland's Anniviers valley near Saint-Luc. The region was a mountain biker's paradise, featuring adrenaline-pumping narrow paths that wound through deep valleys dusted with snow even during summer months.

Lea had sustained a bruise and a slight cut from the fall earlier, halfway through the biking trip. She treated her injuries with a tiny device called *UltRx*, which looked much like a Star Trek Tricorder—almost the same size and very handy. Lea applied infrared radiation to her now-closed wound. UltRx also allowed users to browse the body's various health readings through holographic displays. She was feeling better within five minutes. Soon after Lin confirmed the wound status, they both continued and finished their biking trip.

Lin was Lea's constant companion on outdoor adventures, joining her for activities like hiking, trekking, biking, and rock climbing. Both possessed the physical and mental fitness needed for such demanding adventure sports. Also, forty-two, Lin hailed from Guangzhou, China, but had made France her home for the past thirty-two years. The two had been inseparable since grade school, studying together through college. As nonbinary partners, Lea and Lin were planning to formalize their bond through a HappyChoice relationship, a legal family structure recognized in New-Way countries. They planned to adopt six children, three boys and three girls, each from one of the six inhabited continents.

She was joining others at the Hôtel Weisshorn in the area. The bike was powered by a hydrogen fuel cell and equipped with self-balancing technology. Lea jumped off the bike, which kept full vertical position and balanced on its own, on two wheels without requiring a bike stand.

Lea and Lin went into the hotel to meet with locals who had gathered there along with Mr. Alpean.

"How are you doing, Alpean?" asked Lea.

"I'm doing great, Lea. My training class schedules are fully booked in advance for summer and winter seasons," said Alpean, who ran a training institute for balcony trails and skiing.

Alpean and a group of volunteers were working on a project that surveyed and recorded basic human thoughts and instincts during varied human interactions.

"Alpean's method has a strong emphasis on Humanology and has captured many nuanced interactions in this gigantic survey," Lea thought.

"The purpose of the recordings is to demonstrate how people, when interacting with each other, feel about their levels of willingness to be at their best, present their intentions, and offer lasting experiences to each other," Alpean added.

Lea mentioned that young Araho, Adit's son, was developing a device capable of predicting human reactions based on intentions and delivering real-time cues in social situations. She suggested that Alpean contact Araho to explore whether that research and technology could help with his own survey project.

"Yes, I'll get in touch with Araho. That's exactly what I need!" Alpean said.

The survey considered both first-person and remote interactions. By the 22nd century, many people lived remotely for their entire lives without much personal interactions except for the New-Way education system, which made personal interactions mandatory for children in grade school years. For many, this survey study seemed rather ironic since people today in the early 22nd century don't cherish much personal interactions nor look forward to such encounters.

"People avoid personal encounters with each other as if they're in pandemic times," Alpean joked.

"How are your friends?" Lea asked.

"You mean the LENA Team?" replied Alpean, giving the team a nickname—an acronym for its members Liam, Emma, Noah, and Ava.

"They're fine and waiting to meet you this evening at the hotel conference room," said Alpean. "Liam and Emma got married the HappyChoice way. They're planning to move to Tibet and raise children there. Noah and Ava, along with their friends, have joined masters' programs in Sociology and Humanology at the University of Lucerne in Switzerland."

"Very good! How's your project going?" Lea asked, knowing Alpean is a garrulous talker.

"It's going great and I'm almost finishing up! The team is still in high spirits even after so much hardship endured during the Survey," Alpean said. "Satellite internet helped to seamlessly connect with the global population. The internet is available through space satellites and ground-based 6G cellular services, which improved connectivity and communications."

Alpean and his team had surveyed almost one million respondents, both remote and in first-person interviews. They completed the remote survey and were nearing completion of the field survey part. This was where Alpean wanted to use Araho's device for capturing the intricacies of human behaviors. Alpean, Lea, and others collaborated to create survey feedback models using which they would derive conclusions. These models were being scrutinized closely and were readied for analysis with the Core Team this evening.

Alpean felt a surge of confidence because he believed in his team's innovative survey methods and findings about how people interact in current times. He was thankful to Lea, Grace, Adit, and other key players, including the local university's humanities teaching staff and students.

Lea explained to the group that *the Book*'s relevance to current-day societies was immediate, compelling, and lasting. Vish recognized that among many ways of leading daily lives, physical work had a crucial and prominent part. Everyone should do some daily physical work like gardening, cooking, farming, or other chores. It was also important to include weekly time for Yoga, Tai Chi, Qigong, or similar practices involving stretches, strengths and weights for health benefits of body and mind.

Recognized as a world-renowned human geographer, Dr. Lea extensively studied the interrelationships between people, places, and environments, focusing on how these relationships vary spatially and temporally across and between locations. The interdependence and mutual influence of environmental conditions on living were central to Lea's "Theory of Social Everything." It combined Humanology and Geography (Human Geography) with Psychology.

She drew heavily from *the Book* and its chapters "Reign of Religion" and "Nuances of Human Geography." In the chapter "Reign of Religion" Vish described how sociology, economics, politics and spirituality were intertwined and shaped by the human urge to survive and flourish. She opined, "A broader context allows for consideration of the varied social, economic, and political consequences to derive appropriate perspectives and attain peaceful co-existence."

Lea dealt with the evolutionary course of social actions in her "Theory of Social Everything" by threading together various theories from philosophers such as Auguste Comte, Max Weber, Karl Marx, Émile Durkheim, Michel Foucault, and Erving Goffman.

Lea was committed to maintaining effective communications while applying New-Way Ideology, which was important for both influencers and the general population. It was crucial that people clearly understood the intentions behind these communications and not misinterpret or misapply them, regardless of whether interactions were in-person or remote, or whatever cultures they belonged to. Lea and Alpean recognized the significant role influencers played in this context and planned to present several solutions at that evening's Core meeting.

Lea thought, "When people see the benefits of interaction, they will be more inclined to participate willingly." She was aware of the device Araho was developing, which aimed to solve the conundrum of understanding true human intentions in interactions.

It was time for the meeting of the Core.

Lea, Alpean, and his team went into a room in the hotel to meet with The Core. They pulled out the CommBox gadgetry to join the meeting. They all wore special glasses that securely let them view and decipher the images. Without these glasses, when looking at the holographic message, all one sees is just a beam of light not much different from a flashlight beam.

Kirl

Kirl was a tall and burly man at forty-six years of age. He stood almost six feet four inches and was evidently heavyset. He was a well-known mathematician and philosopher from St. Petersburg, Russia, identifying himself with the St. Petersburg-Leningrad Mathematical School. His name was Dr. Kirl Unyakovsky. He was lovable and always seen with his dog, a male Siberian Husky named Sibsky. Kirl had found the husky when he was just two months old, abandoned on the streets in Moscow suburbs. This puppy belonged to the Spitz genetic family, a working dog breed with an Agouti color.

Kirl had two beautiful daughters, Seva and Reva, from his marriage to Eva. They were identical twins aged seventeen. Kirl had experienced a devastating family tragedy. His wife Eva had died in an accident ten years ago. When it happened, all four family members were returning home from a local children's fair about ten kilometers away on a hill. It was twilight and about to get dark. Kirl had just navigated downhill through two bends down the road, still at the top of the hill, when a medium-sized truck coming up in the opposite direction lost control and hit his car on the passenger side. The truck fell into the gorge and disappeared before Kirl's eyes. His wife died instantly from the crash. The girls were then studying in second grade. Since then, Kirl had help from his mother until the girls graduated from high school.

Kirl was visiting London amidst the chaos. He brought Sibsky, his pet dog. Kirl conducted himself awkwardly in social gatherings and didn't enjoy those settings. However, the philosopher in him was well-versed in debates. He had published many peer-reviewed research findings and presented them at international forums. He didn't love attention, often refusing to accept awards in the past.

There were activists and vigilantes fighting corruption and other social ills in London and other prominent cities in the UK and Europe. There was huge outcry about the degenerate state of governance. Corruption, deception, and selfishness ran rampant in British society, just as in many other countries. Prevailing laws were challenged in courts and on the streets. To the dismay of law-abiding citizens, even some enacted laws were unjust, harmful, discriminatory, or served special interests at the expense of the general population. People wanted New-Way Governance to take over in the UK. Kirl said that Vish's ideas from *the Book* were always in the minds of people wanting change in these unfair times.

Kirl had a meeting with a few of the open supporters in London who are influencers and even vigilantes. The meeting took place in a public library in central London. Kirl spoke about Fair Governance aspects that could apply to the UK and other European nations. Kirl was multilingual, fluent in Russian, Mandarin, Spanish, Hindi, and English. While giving lectures and presentations, he engaged various ethnic groups in their local languages. Kirl connected instantly to people. He was always honest, which made people comfortable with his presence.

"You're a very welcome figure in this community!" Kirl said to Ms. Reeve, from Spain, a prominent figure in the meetings of New-Way support group in London.

"People are genuinely afraid to openly voice dissent against current regimes and their leaders. But I get it—they love me and my friends who are in this with me. Thanks to

Vish's ideologies! People love us even though many of us aren't from here," responded Reeve.

"Vish's ideas and thoughts are very relevant to current-day societies," Reeve added.

Reeve and Krishna, both twenty-four years old, were Ph.D. students from Oxford University researching politics-administration dichotomy.

"Governance in Greater UK reeks of corruption, and people's well-being isn't a priority. The oligarchy's interest weighs highest in budgetary allocations. That's why people love Vish's ideas about Fair Governance," said Krishna, an Indian-origin researcher.

This group and others across England, Wales, Scotland, and Northern Ireland were emboldened by the latest New-Way achievements in Sri Lanka, Slovenia, and other countries. They knew that Kirl and other members of Vish's Core Team were key change agents in Sri Lanka's transformation. Kirl was instrumental in working out various spiritual mechanisms concerning politics, economy, and society with a local hue.

Kirl chose the mix of rational and spiritual temper as the medium for educating the masses.

"Vish was a big supporter of the selfless lifestyle, where selfishness takes the backseat. It takes courage to put oneself aside and bring others' benefits to the front and center," Kirl said to the gathering.

Kirl was the key speaker at symposia and conferences on formal sciences such as Mathematics, Astronomy, and Philosophy. Kirl spoke eloquently in didactic tones but touched the heartfelt feelings of attendees, as shown by swarms of people looking to meet with him personally right after sessions.

Kirl helped set up observatories and planetariums in many cities. These centers had various science pavilions highlighting fundamental realities of nature. They explained creature evolution, extinction, and everything in between across millennia. He was currently working on Science Centers in Australia, China, and India. Kirl knew the theory, attributed to Stephen Hawking, which predicted "the end of the universe" and that Cosmology as a discipline would soon be dead. But Kirl would cheekily say we still had a few million years more to peer through the skies with ever distancing galaxies.

Kirl loved the Science Center he helped set up in Ljubljana, Slovenia's capital and its largest city. The Science Center sat on the banks of the Ljubljanica River near the stem of Tromostovje (Triple Bridge) on the south side. This was in fact the first such center Kirl helped build.

The local government in Ljubljana donated land and provided materials, utilities, and landscaping. Kirl himself architected this planetarium/observatory. He created the science facility with children and common people in mind. Everyone entering these facilities was transported to the medium of scientific temper and inquisitive learning. Every day, they conducted live science demonstrations covering basic science experiments. This aspect of the Science Center was so popular that many people from around the world visited Ljubljana.

Kirl designed the Science City structure to resemble an octopus with eight arms and two legs. The structure appeared to stand on two legs fashioned as rockers and balanced itself dynamically. Each arm housed one of the eight branches of science:

Physics: The study of matter, energy, and fundamental forces of nature

Chemistry: The study of substances, their properties, and how they interact and change

Biology: The study of living organisms, their life processes, and environmental interactions

Earth Science: The study of Earth, its structure, processes, and atmosphere, including geology, meteorology, and oceanography.

Astronomy: The study of celestial bodies, space, and the universe beyond Earth's atmosphere

Mathematics: While often considered a tool for other sciences, it explores numerical relationships, structures, and patterns

Social Sciences: The study of human behavior and societies, including arts, psychology, sociology, anthropology, geography, and economics.

Environmental Science: The study of interactions between physical, chemical, and biological components of the environment, often focusing on human impacts.

The building was an architectural marvel, with each branch extending almost 100 feet outward from the center. The rooms and hallways met all required acoustic standards, and the natural lighting provided adequate illumination during the daytime. The autarkic structure generated renewable energy and kept 100 percent independence with a zero-carbon footprint. The central part housed an enormous dome on the top floor serving as a 5,000-seat planetarium. This was the world's biggest Science Center, with about two million square feet of built-up area and marvelous science demonstration stations.

The Science City had a comprehensive library, second only to the Library of Congress in Washington D.C. However, it had more diverse formats and platforms than Washington's. It supported a huge catalog of art & literature including books in print, digital, holographic, and AR/VR formats. There was instant translation from any language to any other language. Kirl and Adit worked together on this project to fulfill translation tasks.

This library also boasted a huge catalog of music from around the world. Kirl loved music and especially loved music with the instrument *Veena.* He had a penchant for playing Carnatic music from South India. He loved songs that portrayed love amidst contemporary social issues. Kirl ensured the library offered a complete spectrum of world music: folklore, tribal traditions, modern compositions, and space-age creations. This library was also big on art curation. One could find artworks from different millennia. Kirl, with help from the Core Team, digitized entire collections and stored them at different space colonies too for the future.

It was time for the meeting of the Core.

Kirl and his team, including Reeve and Krishna, found a room in that Central London Library to take part in the Core meeting. They pulled out the CommBox to join. The CommBox automatically and appropriately attuned to the respective privileges of the user.

Grace

Grace was a fifty-two-year-old Namibian woman, scholarly with formal and advanced learning in Life Sciences and Genetics. She was a member of the Core CHEFS team. She had authored several peer-reviewed scientific papers on genetic preservation, climate change, and extraterrestrial human habitation. Grace marveled that, even after more than a century of relentless attempts, Mars still defied colonization. This she attributed to the inability of human biology to sustain non-earth environments.

Grace had married at age twenty-one to Chandi Das, a South Asian Indian Telugu-speaking man. She met him during her master's program at the University of the Witwatersrand in Johannesburg. Grace and Chandi Das had three daughters together. Their eldest daughter passed grade school and was now attending her 1st year undergraduate program at a local college. Their marriage lasted twenty years before they divorced by mutual consent, maintaining an amicable relationship. Chandi Das retained custody of their daughters. Since he was a professor at a local Johannesburg college, he could focus on their education and career development while Grace concentrated on global New-Way CHEFS implementations.

Grace was looking at little John playing with other kids in a small Modenso Park outside the capital Bloemfontein, South Africa. John's body above the waist was perfect, but from below the waist, he had severe underdevelopment due to a horrific disease contracted as an infant. The cause remained unknown, with no cure found yet.

Jennifer Crowley—Jen to everyone—watched her son John clapping excitedly and giggling as other children played in the field. Though wheelchair-bound and unable to join them directly, John was fully included in their games. The children naturally accepted his immobility, regularly coming over to pass him the ball and take turns playing with him. Jen felt deeply grateful for their empathy, kindness, and natural inclusiveness.

"The kids are thrilled to play when they have parents present around the corner of their eyes," said Jen.

"That's right," Grace nodded in agreement.

"How's Jack doing? I knew he was on a business trip to New York City," Grace asked. Jack Bowery was John's dad and Jennifer's husband.

"Oh, Jack's fine. He's coming back to Bloemfontein this weekend," Jen answered.

After about an hour of chatting with Jen and other parents, Grace said goodbyes and left the playground.

Grace left for the Coffee House across the street on Rhyn Avenue to meet with Dr. YoloMunk. YoloMunk liked this coffee house for its finest coffee sourced from across Africa. YoloMunk was seated already and waiting for Grace.

Dr. Grace regarded YoloMunk as an exceptionally promising—a twenty-five-year-old woman with wisdom beyond her years. Originally from Sri Lanka, the beautiful South Asian Island nation, YoloMunk was now a licensed physician in the United States, completing a genetics fellowship in Washington, DC.

She had traveled to Cape Town for the International Conference on Medical and Biosciences (ICMBS), which focused on genetics and space radiation's long-term effects on human physiology. Upon the conference's conclusion, YoloMunk flew directly to Bloemfontein to meet with Grace—a meeting she had carefully planned months in advance, knowing they would discuss a potentially groundbreaking genetic disorder case study.

"Dr. YoloMunk is so young, so smart, and so powerful! She's the daughter I never had but always wanted," thought Grace.

At the Coffee place, Grace ordered orange juice and YoloMunk an Ethiopian Yirgacheffe Coffee. Grace requested in-place ground coffee for YoloMunk, who liked it most for its purity, fragrance, and fresh flavor. Over late afternoon beverages, they spent considerable time chatting about diverse topics including genetic mutation, gene therapy, and Brain-Computer Interface (BCI).

Grace insistently brought up her excursion a couple of months ago to birdwatching with Adit, studying birds while flying midair alongside them.

They flew along the 100th meridian boundary in the USA that passes through North Dakota, South Dakota, Nebraska, Kansas, Oklahoma, and Texas—America's breadbasket until the end of the 21st century. With climate change, it wasn't America's breadbasket anymore. Adit maintained VFR flight procedures along that 2,000-mile stretch over approximately five days.

Refueling was kept minimal as in-flight power generation helped recharge batteries. Grace took pictures and videos with her camera and drones perched atop the plane. She could record birds' behavior while keeping eye contact with them in mid-flight. Grace watched and noted birds in flight with Adit piloting a two-seater electric-engine airplane. Adit a few times landed on water, sand dunes and grass fields for close encounters with the avifauna.

Grace's hobby was studying how geography shapes migratory bird routes. YoloMunk could see Grace's excitement while explaining the mid-flight bird watching and studying experiences.

"I learned there are more migratory birds passing through eastern U.S. than western U.S. No places in the West can match the numbers and species of migrant bird flocks found at places like Duluth, Minnesota, or Cape May, New Jersey," Grace said.

Playfully, YoloMunk interjected that the 100th meridian line goes from pole to pole, traced from Manitoba to Mexico in the Americas. She was showing off her geographical knowledge! YoloMunk felt thrilled by Grace's presence, comforted with a sense of belonging.

Once finishing their beverages, they both went to Grace's place about a kilometer away on foot. It was a rather small-looking apartment from outside.

"How's John responding to experimental medication to improve mobility in his lower body?" asked Dr. YoloMunk.

She was studying John's case. The young doctor had invested heavily in gene therapy research for John's sake. She knew John's family was extremely poor and struggling to pay the bills for the treatment. This disease afflicting John had affected quite a few young children in varied populations and geographies. Dr. YoloMunk had exchanged notes about the case with Dr. Grace. She earlier presented this case to her superiors at the university in the USA and developed some ideas.

"Not so great. John's now on the second level of drug administration," said Grace, feeling sorry.

"We don't know yet if methods of drug administration matter. So far there've been no side effects, but we're disappointed that this approach isn't working, and we've lost a couple of months already," Grace continued.

"But the newer method introduces genetically modified single-cell organisms to react with target cells in the patient's lower body. We're hoping this innovative approach will work," Grace told YoloMunk.

We used improved genetic algorithms, generated and applied using more powerful computers. Hopefully, it'll achieve better results within the next few weeks. These methods worked 100 percent favorably on mice and other animal test subjects," YoloMunk acknowledged.

"Yes, I hope this time the drug works!" YoloMunk said.

Grace then retired to her routine for the night. She started reading Vish's book from a random chapter as usual. "New-Way Ideologies brought out the positive effects of rapid changes in life. Socio-cultural paradigm shifts are rapidly happening, especially in smaller countries across the world. The populations in bigger countries are only eager to follow," she mused.

While Grace retired and took a break, YoloMunk went to her own room that Grace allocated for her. YoloMunk read some research topics and updated notes on John Crowley Bowery.

After two hours of well-deserved rest, they were energized and gathered again—it was time to meet with the Core Team. They walked into the adjacent laboratory, which was not noticeably big but equipped with powerful scientific equipment. A few devices there monitored changes in DNA and RNA in response to medication, while other instruments induced changes to DNA and RNA strands. Grace was researching how to remove and replace inferior DNA and RNA segments that had evolved since Neanderthal times.

It was now time to meet with Core.

Grace, with her assistants and YoloMunk, gathered around to meet The Core. They pulled out gadgetry to join the meeting. All wore glasses to read secure holostream messages during the meeting.

Sparq

Ms. Sparq, about forty-five years old but looking much younger, worked part-time at Tyb Alqalb International Hospital, one of Dubai's biggest and best hospitals. She was the majority shareholder of the hospital system—a fact few people knew. She was a member of the Core CHEFS team.

Ms. Sparq belonged to a wealthy Emirati family from Abu Dhabi and was heir to an enormous fortune, which she intended to use for noble causes. She was a philanthropist and influencer, translating thoughts into actions with unwavering commitment to humanism. She handpicked global causes such as climate, equality, science education, and healthcare. She served on the boards of her projects.

Under her direct-help programs, she funded projects for food, health, and shelter for the needy and offered work opportunities at her philanthropic organizations. Under her indirect-help programs, she also funded global projects run by other non-profits, including R&D organizations for climate change and genetic research. Ms. Sparq also supported NGOs and advocacy groups that championed balanced social development across global regions, and funded activism aimed at restoring the humanistic values that were central to New-Way ideology.

"Hey, Sparqly!" The children in the lobby spotted her and shouted in exhilaration as she entered the hospital.

She was none other than the central figure of the hospital and a member of UAE royalty, Ms. Yasmin Al Nahyan. Fondly known as Ms. Sparq, she radiated joy and boundless energy as she dealt with patients. The nickname 'Sparq' stuck with her. Despite her royal background, she insisted on serving as a nurse—a commoner role. Her smile was electrifying, honest, and heartening. She was always jovial, earning her the affectionate nickname Sparqly from kids.

She was beloved by patients and their attendants alike. Adults marveled at her grace and boundless energy, particularly when tending to sick children. She personally ensured every patient received comprehensive medical and art care along with emotional support. Her arsenal of gentle humor and clever quips could win over even the most challenging patients, bringing smiles to faces throughout the ward.

Ms. Sparq had donated a generous sum rumored to be the majority stake of the hospital's equity. Early in her tenure, she worked in Cardiology and Emergency Care divisions. For the past couple of years, she'd been in the Children's Care unit, which boasted the world's largest number of beds for children. She ensured she always served in non-VIP care units, sought after by poorer sections of the population due to affordability. She would serve where it mattered most!

Vish stayed a constant presence in her thoughts and actions. His book provided her with peace of mind and clear guidance toward a bright, calm existence, free from chaos. His fundamental insight that joy and suffering were inextricably woven into the human condition resonated profoundly with her own experiences.

Ms. Sparq believed in Vish's idea that humans, despite their contradictory tendencies, would not be self-destructive in the end—though that was something to be wary of. The potential for self-destruction weighed heavily on Vish's mind, leading him to devise methods of motivation for positive deeds and deterrents for harmful ones. The LifeScore mechanism, along with the New-Way Justice System, aimed to ensure humanity's well-being equitably and sustainably. Ms. Sparq herself was very positive and boldly optimistic about human actions for their own well-being.

That morning, Sparq dealt with an eleven-year-old patient, Lucas, being treated for a rare cancer variant. He looked physically frail but proven unyielding mental strength, which she knew would be his salvation as he unfortunately transitioned into stage 3.

"Hey Lucas, my young man! How are you doing this morning?" Ms. Sparq greeted him as she entered the room.

"Hey, Sparqly! Good morning! You're on time! Look what I got yesterday evening from my friend Atif—a fidget spinner that creates holographic 3D figures using laser beams," Lucas shouted feebly.

"Look, I can switch between 3D symbols from a Cross to a Crescent Moon with a star to an Om symbol to a Dharma chakra," he explained breathlessly.

The symbolism wasn't lost on Sparq. She was amazed by Lucas's ability to navigate different religious symbols with such maturity. She laughed, acknowledging and appreciating it, and asked if she could try. Lucas gave it to her at once with a wide smile stretching across his face as he basked in her appreciation. Lucas rarely let anyone else play with that toy, but Ms. Sparq was special to him.

After checking Lucas's vitals, Ms. Sparq gave him a dry bath, changed his clothes and bed sheets, and tucked him back into bed. Lucas managed to eat breakfast with some difficulty while Ms. Sparq watched and talked to him. His breakfast consisted of easily digestible natural food and a half-cup of freshly squeezed orange juice.

Ms. Sparq tidied the room, knowing Lucas's parents would visit soon. And soon they arrived along with Lucas's friend Atif. The steady interaction with Ms. Sparq helped the family and friends cope with Lucas's trauma. It was hard on all of them. After speaking with the doctors, Lucy and Luther, Lucas's parents, vented their concerns to Ms. Sparq, who listened with patience, empathy and kindness.

"Ms. Sparq, will he get rid of the malignancy and go back to Stage 2?" asked Lucy herself, a cancer survivor. She had asked this question countless times.

"Lucy, Luther, there's hope and every possibility that Lucas gets back to remission and normalcy. He just needs more time with new medication and treatment methods. The good thing is, he's young and still has time," Sparq reassured them.

"Lucas is a brave young man!" Sparq said.

She mentioned Dr. YoloMunk was on the case. Lucy and Luther felt reassured, knowing Dr. YoloMunk's credentials and dedication to their case to the profession.

Ms. Sparq and Ms. Grace, both members of the New-Way CHEFS team, collaborated on healthcare projects involving cancer research with a focus on genetics. These four—including YoloMunk and AJ—collaborated on treatment options for cancer patients. AJ proposed a plan to administer cancer drugs to include all sections of beneficiary patients equitably.

Under the Al Sharara Foundation, Ms. Sparq established many organizations, including educational and philanthropic institutions. These institutions offered Science & Spiritual education globally, from grade school to college research studies, with tie-ups with eminent institutions worldwide. Genetics, Automation, AI, and Climate research received a major share of her funds.

Afia Jawahra, called AJ, was thirty-two years old. She confronted and fought against inequality, challenging it in various forms like classism, sexism, racism, and other segregation methods. She spoke out against these practices in diverse public settings. Sparq recognized AJ's commitment and steadfastness and made her in charge of a couple of institutions. AJ headed Alkadir Almusawat Waleadala, a non-profit organization founded by Ms. Sparq based on Vish's principles of Equality and Justice. AJ managed this organization, overseeing close to USD 2 billion, collaborating with volunteers and global players.

It was time for the meeting of the Core.

Sparq, AJ, and the team gathered in a meeting room in the hospital building to join the Core meeting. They pulled out necessary gadgets to connect.

**

The New-Way path forward

The New-Way Ideology from *the Book* served as a life guide for its followers. The book was relatively small, containing only about fifty pages. Followers believed this book had changed the world forever—yet again, a once-in-a-millennium occurrence.

The year was in the early 22nd century, and times were chaotic politically and socially on a global scale. Massive changes swept through all levels of society, essentially driven by the transformative New-Way Ideology. People reflected on the long history of humankind, pondering what lay ahead as they yearned for a fair and brighter future.

The Justice System reigned supreme above all other governance systems, using the LifeScore mechanism & CHEFS policies to guarantee equitable governance. Central to Vish's revolutionary teachings was a transformative vision of social justice: "*the practice of a society where everyone is accorded equal judicial, economic, political, social, and spiritual rights and opportunities.*" Until now this concept had become virtually meaningless in most nations, but Vish's ideology rekindled its power, resonating deeply with populations worldwide who had grown weary of oppressive leadership, including supposedly democratic governments that concentrated power and privilege in the hands of an elite few.

"The consequences of the imbalance have exacted an unacceptably cruel human toll which simply has to be stopped," declared Vish. Under New-Way doctrine, the essence of Life itself was redefined as the Sum of its Actions with consequences. The groundbreaking LifeScore system proved remarkably effective in the early years of its adoption in the New-Way countries.

For people everywhere to embrace the life-changing values of the New Age doctrine, two critical conditions had to be met without compromise.

First, they had to be convinced of the personal rewards, incentives, and recognition this new way of life offered them. At the most basic level, human nature still responds best to things that serve personal interests.

Second, there also had to be real consequences and penalties when individuals crossed the sacred lines of ethical behavior and human decency.

The LifeScore metric accomplished this dual mandate—serving as a powerful incentive for adherents while simultaneously disincentivizing non-compliant individualistic tendencies in a subtle yet powerful way.

Vish's vision was for governance with justice, economy with balance, society with equality, and spirituality with peace.

Many among Vish's inner circle were positioned at the forefront of these global endeavors—the indefatigable activist Ms. Maria, the edgy economist Mr. Adit, the fiery social reformer Ms. Lea, the erudite philosopher Mr. Kirl, the brilliant geneticist Dr. Grace, and the benevolent Emirati humanitarian Ms. Sparq. Using New-Way ideologies, they touched all aspects of life—politics, administration, economy, culture, society, and spirituality. These extraordinary individuals and countless others were selflessly dedicated to instituting the New-Way tenets across societies, cultures, and geopolitical fault lines.

Now that we've met the Core Team, let us witness how these stalwarts breathe life into four realms of change: the judicial, the political, the economic, and the social—all bound by spirituality—not as mere concepts but as lived practice.

***

Politics and Administration

It was the end of 21st century and beginning of 22nd century, marking the dawn of the New-Way Ideology era.

Most widely recognized global democracies of the 21st century had governance models comprising Legislative, Executive, Judicial, and optionally Electoral branches. However, these political systems often overshadowed and dominated the other branches, leading to a shift from democratic governance toward oligarchies, pseudo-feudal systems, or even autocracies. In the face of democracy's decline, Vish envisioned a renaissance of true democracy through New-Way Governance. This visionary framework rests on four pillars—Judicial, Diplomatic, Executive, and Electoral—with spirituality serving as both guide and guardian."

The judicial system was at the pinnacle and had oversight over all other governance systems. The New-Way Judicial System fostered equal opportunity, ensured fairness both in principle and practice, upheld accountability, and embraced acceptance of differing viewpoints. The New-Way system facilitated the dichotomy of politics and administration where national administration looked after internal execution branches and international administration looked after global collaboration with diplomacy.

The below schematic illustrates the New-Way governance framework:

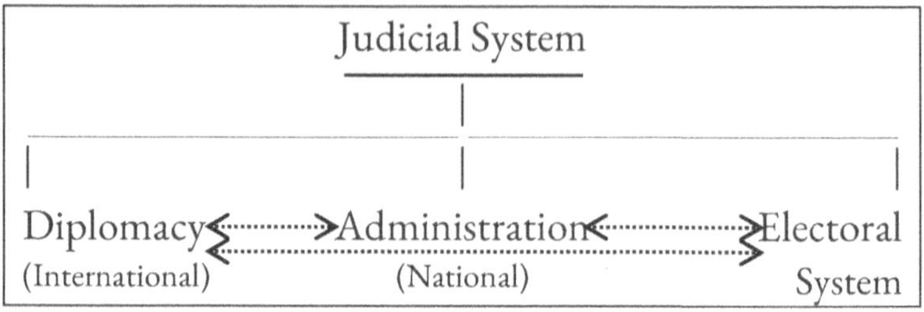

This governance model elevated the judicial system to an apex organization while separating politics from administration. The judiciary served as guardians of law, order, and individual rights while also writing laws. Quasi-elected councils at various levels establish implementation policies according to these laws and executed them within their jurisdictions. This framework enhanced accountability and efficiency through separation of powers, keeping governance simple and local. Vish believed this model would create a more balanced, effective system with truly enforceable checks and balances.

The influencer-catalyst Ms. Maria, the Core member, led the global efforts to implement New-Way Governance.

Maria and her arch-nemesis

Maria was meeting today with Sreeman Divyanshu, an Indian American currently living in Los Angeles and a top key representative from Leviat Sata Group (LSG). Sreeman hoped to dissuade Maria from propagating the dichotomy of Administration and Politics even outside New-Way countries. This group saw the dangers of New-Way Governance spreading across countries even if in parts. Sreeman saw Maria's ever-growing influence in the Americas and was wary of his group losing economic and political influence. The New-Way Ideologies, when implemented, would separate politics from administration and bring every action under judicial scope. This dichotomy would cause the current political system to lose prevalent administrative leverage and hence lose political and monetary advantages.

Mr. Sata, whose real name was *Leviat Sata*, founded the renowned Leviat Sata Group and vetted this summit. Sata was a 50+ year old elusive figure, just like Vish. It was an interesting coincidence that both these elusive global figures were contemporaries, wielded enormous influence on societies, and polarized the entire world. They held diametrically opposing views and even symbolically hailed from antipodal cities. While Sata, now settled in Sri Lanka, amassed huge wealth, Vish, reportedly living in Nepal, had no wealth to mention. Nobody knew if they ever interacted, adding to the mysteries surrounding their personalities.

Sata needed no introduction. He was a lone multi-trillionaire and the world's wealthiest individual. He was the backbone of many global governments. Sata Resources Corporation, another conglomerate belonging to him, was a mining monopoly business with terrestrial and outer space mining operations. It had multi-trillion US dollar mining operations on asteroids, in near-Earth orbits, and on minor planets from the main asteroid belt such as Ceres,

Vesta, Pallas, and Hygiea. The corporation mined precious metals such as gold, silver, platinum group metals, and iron group metals, used for mega-constructions in space. However, Sata's group was particularly interested in C-type, or carbonaceous asteroids due to their carbon-rich minerals, including water. These asteroids met all human exploration needs for essential supplies in space, providing carbon minerals ranging from life-supporting elements to infrastructure-creating materials.

Sata's followers considered Maria's activism—and its influence on affluent sovereign nations—to be dangerous. They knew that embracing New-Way Governance would shatter the global dominance of wealthy, powerful countries controlled by the ultra-rich elite. The meeting was happening at Sreeman's palatial building overlooking Malibu beach. Maria with her small team arrived in a hovercraft and disembarked close to the seating area. From that meeting area, they could see the beach in full expansive view. They noted the heavy security. Maria thought that the more power and riches amassed, the more insecure one becomes.

Maria's team had initially proposed a remote meeting using holographic technology. However, Maria herself intervened to have an in-person meeting to dispel Sreeman's unfounded aspirations of swaying the Core Team to Sata's side. One could discern the palpable tension between followers of each side about the outcome of this meeting, the consequence of the ideological divide between Sata's deviance and Vish's ideals.

Maria was accompanied by Mr. Raj Malorta and Ms. Pame Alverez representing the Core Team. On this early fall afternoon, they were seated under a gazebo-style canopy facing the ocean. It was bright with a cool breeze on the shore—a perfect setting for an afternoon summit. Sreeman's human staff served light drinks to the guests, a rare in the age of robot helpers.

Sreeman Divyanshu approached with folded hands, his two Fox Hounds leading the way. The well-groomed dogs seemed to introduce their master to Maria. Sreeman was tall, handsome, and dark-skinned, with an infectious grin and affable disposition. He was multilingual, fluent in Chinese, Hindi, English, and Spanish. Yet nothing about his lifestyle appeared ordinary to onlookers or by official records. His reputation included covering up misdeeds, illicit relationships, money laundering, and even murder charges by corrupting political and administrative bodies. Sreeman wielded the wealth and power typical of those in the top echelons of the Leviat Sata Group. He was accompanied by Mr. Stephen Vic and Ms. Jacky Brown.

Maria was slightly distracted by the aura and splendor of Sreeman's entry and his infectious charm. They greeted and exchanged pleasantries in Spanish, then quickly settled into the agenda. The atmosphere was palpably taut with teasing conversations as each tried to influence the other. They got down to business at once, wasting no time.

Sreeman, in an exquisite stentorian voice, said, "Hey Odd, hey Evn, come say hello to our guest Maria." Odd and Evn were the names of Sreeman's pet dogs. Odd was male and Evn the female. The dogs came a few steps closer toward Maria and sat upright as if saying a warm hello.

"Hey guys, you're very cute!" Maria said while noticing Sreeman's arrogance and petted them lovingly.

"Maria, don't you think Autonomous Budgetary Allocation is inefficient and prone to hacking? I know this is deep tech stuff, but disruptive actors could hack and subvert your intentions," Sreeman started the conversation.

He knew Adit was behind this technology and had built the solution using triumvirate of advanced technologies, making the process highly efficient and unhackable.

"Sreeman, I'm glad you asked. We're using advanced post-quantum cryptography that is completely secure against hacking to protect transactions and prevent fraud," Maria said confidently.

"Powerful quantum computers have broken many encryption algorithms," Sreeman remarked skeptically. He wasn't convinced it was hacker-proof.

"The technology is flawless for the near future, relying on quantum key distribution and post-quantum random number generators. Plus, we have added safeguards developed by Adit and team, which make our New-Way Cryptography exceptionally secure," Maria said.

She continued, "While I can't explain all the field implementation details for lack of my understanding, we know of no current or foreseeable technology that can break New-Way Encryption."

She knew Sreeman was powerful and could influence his boss Sata. She was aware he came to buy her out of New-Way Governance implementations. They covered many other aspects of New-Way Politics and Administration and their dichotomy. Maria knew it was difficult to change some practices that were centuries or even millennia old. But she also knew, "*No struggle, no change, and no change, no progress*," as Vish put it.

Sreeman thought talking to Maria felt like they were slowly losing a grip on the status quo. Sreeman knew they had failed to acknowledge New-Way Ideology taking root in smaller countries across the globe under their noses and in plain sight. He thought it was like wildfire needing to be stopped from spreading.

"Maria, you know the Secretary of State of the US isn't pleased with New-Way Ideologies. I could arrange a meeting with staff from the secretary's department or even with the Secretary herself," Sreeman said as a final salvo.

Maria knew this was coming and wasn't surprised by the insinuations and veiled threats.

She said, "Our team could meet with the state department—that's not an issue. However, that won't change my opinions or those of my team. We have shown the world that New-Way Governance works for the well-being of entire populations. Admittedly, these have been small countries so far. But by whichever metrics you care to measure, the population is happy. The implementations have been completely transparent."

Sreeman grew increasingly uneasy, detecting neither positive signals from Maria nor any hope in their conversation.

He said, "The actual test of Vish's ideology is when people embrace it open-heartedly. You don't see that in bigger countries. Instead, you are seeing so much unrest and resistance within these big countries to this fad of Vish's revolutionary New-Way ideas." Sreeman was trying to sow seeds of doubt about hardships ahead for Maria and followers of New-Way Ideology.

To which Maria said that Vish's proposition of the dichotomy of politics and administration was based on people's needs that remained unsatisfied for centuries. This dichotomy of governance differentiated internal versus external focus. Administration took care of people's living needs internally at the micro level while politics took care of diplomacy needs externally at the macro level. The much-clamored change from City-State and Nation-State to the Inter-State political system had already changed the political landscape in New-Way countries Namibia, New Zealand, Dubai (UAE), Slovenia, Sri Lanka, and Uruguay.

Traditional politics aimed to answer, "Who shall make laws?" while traditional administration attempted to address, "How to administer such laws?" In contrast, New-Way Governance aimed to answer, "Who will interact externally on the global platform?" while internal administration attempted to answer, "How to administer automated budgets internally?"

The meeting time of one hour was up. Both parties stood their ground. Both knew the outcome and they did goodbyes with "Namaste," the Indian style of greeting, not agreeing on any items discussed. Sreeman felt lost and defeated in the face of the puny but powerful woman that Maria was.

Autonomy of Administration

The Core Team was the singular and most powerful influencing force for spreading the new age ideology. Each member was a stalwart in their respective fields and respected globally.

Maria and the team laid out blueprints for all aspects of Governance at various organizational levels, with specific goals to achieve true administrative autonomy. Maria recognized that safeguarding administrative independence relied on backing from suitable organizational structures including enforcing agencies, overseen by accountable stewards and subject to independent electoral and judicial review.

For administrative agencies to perform their functions efficiently and effectively without external interference, they needed transparent access to independent and trustworthy field data and consequent independent and autonomous budgetary allocations. The crucial field data was collected using Internet Things (IoT) sensors that captured information in real-time in multiple forms and formats, including audio, video, images, and other complex and heterogeneous information data types. Data accumulation and preliminary analysis was conducted at field source level. These data metrics helped in mapping and scoring needs and wants for eventual budgetary allocations. Every citizen gave feedback. Community councils did error checking on this field-level reality metrics and corrected for data mistakes.

This was a continuous process, operating 24/7/365 and using robust blockchain technologies to prevent fraud, double allocation, and unauthorized access with federated control. The parameters for human *needs* ranged from personal, societal, administrative, and judicial aspects. The parameters for human *wants* were based on balancing holistic resource usage and ecological balance. Both material and spiritual criteria were factored in and overlaid onto the core field data.

The New-Way Governance guaranteed life's subsistence to all its citizens. It defined subsistence as catering to the basic needs as encapsulated in CHEFS.

Governance had identified support systems ranging from producing goods and services to implementing distribution mechanisms. Governments implemented field infrastructures to capture individual *needs* and calibrate their *wants.* It established institutions that ensured prompt production and distribution of just enough goods and services. There were also guardrails set up to check justifiable consumption levels.

In this New-Way living, everyone had to work, perhaps even work hard, according to their competence and capability. There were various levels and types of work available for people to choose from and take part in. There was a master catalog of tasks that was constantly and transparently updated. People chose work from that task list.

Maria said, "No capable person should live idly on mere CHEFS subsistence. Active participation in work earns positive credits toward their LifeScore, determining their eligibility for further material comforts and benefits beyond basic needs." Maria, along with the Core members, drove Vish's concepts of well-being, which was evolutionary and progressive.

"*Living,*" Vish had stated, "*is not a quest for the meaning of existence, nor is it getting by idly. Living is the practice of making choices and participating in communities every day.*"

Expanding on this, Maria believed, "One should positively choose actions for sustainable progress."

Puerto Vallarta Convention

On this weekend, Maria, Kirl, and Lea were holding a conference at the International Convention Center in Puerto Vallarta, on Mexico's Pacific coast in Jalisco state. The convention aimed to explain New-Way philosophy primarily to the South American population. This event was both in-person and streamed globally. They knew Leviat Sata influence was omnipresent and posed direct hurdles to thwart New-Way movements. That's why the Core Team ensured all their policies were public, transparent, and unambiguous to counter adverse propaganda.

Amanda and Matheus, both from Brazil, were in Puerto Vallarta to meet with Maria and her team before the event. They were employed in the Brazilian government as heads of the traditional Civil-Supply administration branches. They commanded between them entire civil distribution wings for essential food items. They had also served on consulting boards during the political and administrative transition in Uruguay—a significant shift that affected various aspects of life in that country. The transition involved adopting New-Way Governance and various concepts from New-Way Ideology.

Maria could communicate Vish's ideologies easily as select attendees in the pre-event were familiar with ideas from the Book. Attendees were enthusiastic and eager to share New-Way ideas with a broader audience from South American countries.

Maria emphasized that the core of implementing New-Way philosophy lies in how individuals interpret and apply the New-Way's understanding of life. It assigned weights to actions based on whether those were for Self or for Selfless purposes. This formula allowed for material incentives, such as a fancy car, a nicer home, or other non-essential comforts granting luxury and vanity.

The symposium at Puerto Vallarta covered various aspects of independent administration. It was a hectic two-day event with several papers presented, lectures conducted, and convivial group discussions and sessions, all demonstrating the relevance of New-Way philosophy to current times. Amanda and Matheus led several debates, while Maria presented papers and delivered lectures. She emphasized universal well-being as the benefits of New-Way Ideologies and reminded attendees of friction and opposition from status quoists like the Leviat Sata groups.

Amanda and Matheus showcased Uruguay's Governance and shared how its population benefited from changes in social, economic, and political life. The chasm between poor and rich was eliminated by meeting the population's needs and wants according to their deservance using LifeScore method & CHEFS policy. Within a couple of years of adopting Vish's ideologies, people were living healthy lives with respect and dignity. People witnessed ever-reducing inequalities. This transformation in New-Way Uruguay fascinated people from other South American countries, especially in neighboring Brazil, Chile, and Argentina.

As the symposium continued, several topics were addressed, from practical aspects of implementing New-Way Governance to the philosophical underpinnings of Vish's ideology. Discussions included integration of advanced technology with human-centered governance, the role of education in fostering a New-Way society, and the importance of healthcare in ensuring high quality of life for citizens.

One key session focused on the role of technology in New-Way Governance. Adit presented a comprehensive overview of how advanced communication systems, Blockchain, AI, and IoT were being used to create transparent and efficient citizen participation in administration. He highlighted how real-time data and analysis helped leaders and administrators make informed decisions for the people.

Lea presented at a session on societal and cultural policy frameworks. She discussed the application of humanism and consequentialism concepts to create a society valuing hard work, empathy, inclusiveness, and mutual respect. Lea's policies aimed to foster a cultural environment where every individual could thrive, irrespective of background. Her approach was rooted in belief that a society's strength lies in its diversity and ability to harness this diversity for collective growth.

Kirl's session on the intersection of science and spirituality was both enlightening and thought-provoking. He explored how scientific advancements could be harmonized with spiritual growth, creating a balanced approach to human development. Kirl emphasized that technology and spirituality weren't mutually exclusive but could complement each other in achieving a higher state of human existence. His ideas resonated with many of the attendees who saw potential for a more comprehensive approach to personal and societal growth.

Sparq's presentation on healthcare and education was particularly impactful. She outlined a comprehensive plan to overhaul these sectors, ensuring every individual had access to quality healthcare and education. Sparq's policies focused on preventive healthcare, using technology to provide personalized care, and ensuring education was accessible to all, fostering lifelong learning and personal development. Her vision was to create a society where health and knowledge were cornerstones of human development.

Grace's session on health research, climate protection, food production, and life preservation highlighted the importance of sustainability in New-Way Governance. She discussed the need for a proactive approach to environmental protection, emphasizing the interconnectedness of human health and environment. Grace's policies aimed to create a sustainable future where the well-being of the planet and its inhabitants was priority. Her approach was rooted in the belief that preserving the environment was essential for survival and prosperity of future generations.

The symposium also featured interactive sessions where attendees could engage with the Core Team and discuss practical aspects of implementing New-Way Ideology in their own communities and countries.

One interactive session focused on the concept of HappyChoice, the New-Way Relationship model. Attendees were particularly interested in how this model could be integrated into their own societies, replacing traditional marriage with a more flexible, consensual, and responsible approach to relationships. Maria and the team provided detailed explanations of legal and administrative frameworks supporting HappyChoice, as well as benefits it brought in terms of personal freedom and holistic communal well-being.

Another interactive session delved into the mechanics of the LifeScore system, used to reward individuals based on their contributions to society. Maria explained how the system worked, emphasizing higher weightage given to selfless actions. This session sparked lively debate among attendees keen to understand how such a system could be implemented in their own societies and how it could foster a more equitable society.

Throughout the symposium, the Core Team emphasized the importance of transparency and accountability in New-Way Governance. They discussed guardrails to ensure administrative agencies to run in compliance with governance rules and without external or political interferences. Maria highlighted the role of independent judicial reviews and transparent budgetary allocations in supporting integrity of administration at every social level.

The symposium concluded with a panel discussion featuring all Core Team members. They addressed questions from the audience, covering a wide range of topics from philosophical foundations of New-Way Ideology to practical challenges of implementation. The panel discussion was a fitting end to the symposium, providing comprehensive overview of New-Way vision and reinforcing commitment of Core Team to create a better future for humanity.

As attendees left the convention center, there was a palpable sense of optimism and determination. The ideas and concepts discussed over two days resonated deeply with many, and there was ardent desire to take these ideas back to their own countries and begin the process of transformation. Maria, Adit, Lea, Kirl, Sparq, and Grace had successfully communicated Vish's vision, and seeds of New-Way Ideology had been sown in the hearts and minds of attendees.

Inspired by Uruguay's success, other countries in the region, including Brazil, Chile, and Argentina, began adopting similar approaches albeit slowly. In Brazil, the government launched comprehensive review of its administrative systems, looking to implement principles of transparency and accountability. Adit's expertise in technology and communications played a crucial role in this process, with advanced systems being deployed to collect and analyze real-time data. This data was used to make informed decisions, ensuring resources were allocated efficiently and effectively.

Chile and Argentina focused on societal and cultural aspects of New-Way Ideology, using Lea's insights into humanism. Policies were designed to foster inclusivity and mutual respect, creating a cultural environment where every individual could thrive. These policies are supported by robust education systems, as outlined by Sparq, which prioritize knowledge acquisition and personal development.

In Mexico, success of symposium led to renewed commitment to environmental protection. Grace's emphasis on sustainability resonated deeply with policymakers. Initiatives were launched to protect natural habitats, reduce pollution, and promote renewable energy sources, aligning with Grace's vision of sustainable future.

The Core Team's commitment to transparency and accountability ensured that the principles of New-Way Governance were upheld, sustaining a positive impact on society. The road to transformation wasn't without challenges. Groups like Leviat Sata's, representing status quo, continued to pose hurdles, resisting change and trying to undermine the New-Way movement.

The symposium at Puerto Vallarta marked a significant milestone in global implementation of New-Way Ideology. Led by Maria, the Core Team successfully communicated Vish's vision, inspiring attendees from around the world to evince interest in and to embrace principles of New-Way Governance.

(*Puerto Vallarta is in a geographical sweet spot in Mexico—on Mexico's west coast and the Bay of Banderas, the second-largest bay in the world, sheltered by the Sierra Madre Occidental Mountain range, protected from the threat of hurricanes.*)

Decentralization of Governance

The goal of universal decentralization was ambitious yet elegant: to increase citizen participation, enhance individual accountability, improve governance efficiency, and ensure fair access to resources and services. This transformation would foster greater diversity and innovation while creating a fairer distribution of power and resources. The New-Way Governance system allocated budgets strictly based on community needs, with autonomous allocations cross-checked and ratified by constituents in near real-time. This revolutionary implementation relied heavily on technologies developed by Adit and his team—from secure access protocols to advanced cryptography, distributed storage, predictive analysis, and high-bandwidth communication networks.

When asked, "Is it possible to have decentralized governance as a way of governing at the country level?" Maria answered emphatically, "Yes, it is absolutely possible through the delegation of authority and the devolution of power to local governing bodies, such as community and cooperative organizations."

Maria believed governance should avoid concentrating power within a few individuals. This was achievable only by delegating decision-making to local bodies and implementing independent and autonomous budget allocations for various public works. Community, village, county, and state governments needed to function as interconnected cogs in the wheel of federated governance. The New-Way framework featured auto-adjusting funds allocations from local to national levels—allocations that weren't subject to the whims and fancies of any person or group. Only the genuine needs of people influenced budgetary decisions. This mechanism employed autonomous algorithms with active but mandatory feedback from citizens and community councils to balance priorities.

Local governments' role was to distribute tasks among public, private, and hybrid entities for project implementation. Decentralization through delegation and devolution of power operated at political, administrative, monetary and fiscal levels, aimed solely at sustainable and fair governance. The monetary system was largely comprised of self-regulated NeWay Crypto currency supported by LifeScore mechanisms. CHEFS was fully funded and outside of monetary system governance.

Moscow Convergence

Maria had endured a hectic couple of weeks preparing for and attending the Puerto Vallarta Meet. Afterward, she craved rest and quiet time. She wanted to visit Grace in Namibia, spend time with her and her three children, and discuss pandemic administration protocols with Grace's ex-husband—an expert in epidemiology and virology, especially relevant in these times given the recurring nature of deadly pandemics. However, she couldn't make the trip because Kirl had arranged urgent meetings in Moscow. When Kirl organized something, it became priority number one.

Maria flew from Mexico City's Benito Juárez International Airport to Moscow. Kirl met her at Vnukovo International Airport, having chosen it for its proximity to downtown Moscow where local meetings awaited. As Maria emerged from the arrival terminal with her luggage, Kirl stood at the ground transportation level, waving eagerly.

Despite being a skilled Multi Engine Land (MEL) airplane pilot who could have flown himself, Kirl had taken the Sapsan train from St. Petersburg, then cabbed to the airport. Spotting Maria first, he shouted, "Hey Привет, Maria!"

Maria turned toward Kirl's enthusiastic greeting. "Hey there, Kirl!" They exchanged broad grins, thrilled to see each other despite having met just the previous week at Puerto Vallarta's International Convention Center. Their exhilaration transcended mere friendship—it was an ideological bond.

Kirl towered over petite Maria, their size difference making their warm embrace oddly endearing. He took her luggage, loaded it into the waiting taxi, and opened the door for her. Their driver, Enebish, was Mongolian and loved engaging passengers in conversation. Kirl knew him well and had specifically requested his taxi services instead of the autonomous taxi drive.

During the thirty-minute ride from airport to the hotel, Enebish cheerfully shared insights, without anyone asking, into Inner Mongolian culture. He explained that village elders had given him his name, which literally meant "taboo" and was believed to ward off evil. He spoke fondly of Mongolian hospitality as he drove leisurely to their destination—a modest but comfortable hotel with a large hall and attached guest rooms.

Mikhail Smirkhof and Kristina Rivenova received them at the hotel entrance. Both were devoted followers of New-Way ideology and invaluable allies to Kirl. Kristina, originally from Slovenia, had helped Kirl in establishing the observatory/planetarium at Ljubljana's Science Center. Mikhail, a local Muscovite, was both a mathematician and an ambitious greenhouse enthusiast. He cultivated everything needed for Kasha—a nutritious drink made from whole grains including buckwheat, oats, wheat, millet, barley, and rice—at scale across his network of cooperative greenhouses surrounding Moscow metropolitan area.

Mikhail owned Planet Kasha, a restaurant that served free meals to anyone pledging allegiance to New-Way ideology, while others paid cost-covering prices. This policy made him popular throughout Russia and neighboring Eastern European countries. People traveled from afar to obtain his pristine, organic produce and to enjoy healthy meals at Planet Kasha.

Kirl had arranged for local groups to attend private meetings with Maria. After settling into their rooms for a well-deserved rest, they prepared for intensive discussions the following morning. Kirl and his team were tasked with explaining the spiritual aspects of the dichotomy between politics and administration, and the principles of decentralized governance. For the population, this represented an enormous shift away from traditional murky politics, which was power intertwined with administration. Many feared the new system would plunge society into chaos. Kirl and his team took responsibility for explaining New-Way Ideology's benefits and sharing experiences from the six countries that had successfully implemented this dichotomy.

Kirl believed people, in this New-Way transformative era, should shed their fears and trust autonomous processes dedicated to the common good—whether it's in local, city, county, or state level government bodies. Politics in the form of diplomacy would exist only at the Inter-State level for international issues, not within countries. Kirl believed that selfless actions define trust and pave the way for decentralized governance while eliminating the idolatry of privileged elites and countering the entrenched pseudo-feudalism infecting current capitalism.

Approximately 200 people from various Eastern European countries attended the meetings with Maria, Kirl, and their team in person, while many more participated remotely from locations across the region. Kristina and Mikhail personally knew all the attendees. Using a large holographic display, the session presented decentralization concepts in what amounted to a comprehensive train-the-trainers program for future change agents in their respective countries.

Adit, Lea, Sparq, and Grace attended remotely and holographically. The meetings supported an informal structure but rigid focus on outcomes—typical of Russian organizational style, especially under Kirl's leadership. Despite his serious demeanor, attendees recognized Kirl's gentle, kind nature. Maria delivered presentations related to politics and dichotomy to groups from various Eastern European countries eager to understand New-Way Ideologies better, knowing that Maria's teams had successfully implemented these concepts in Uruguay and Sri Lanka.

Kristina and Mikhail shared the practical realities of decentralization with attendees, emphasizing how traditional political leadership would be removed from local decision-making processes. Instead, local administrators would make decisions based on local data, autonomous resource allocations, and direct population feedback. This ended the political interference in local development and progress. This approach stood in stark contrast to existing 21st century systems where politicians influenced outcomes while offering no guarantee of selfless service.

Data that enabled decision-making processes remained accessible online to qualified citizens. This allowed councils and administrators along with every citizen to actively provide feedback. Because raw data was manipulation-resistant, automatic budget allocations based on this unalterable information achieved near-complete impartiality.

Localization through Prime Directive

At the heart of Vish's localization approach lay a simple yet profound principle: those who lived within cultural and community realities had the deepest understanding of them. Vish held an unwavering belief that everyone deserved the freedom to choose their cultural journey and embrace it with dignity. The concept was inherently personal and local rooted in the power of people and communities to decide their own destinies.

Earlier in that week, before the Puerto Vallarta symposium, Amanda, Maria and a few others flew into Montevideo the capital city of Uruguay. Amanda had taken Maria and others to Montevideo's local Carnival in Uruguay. The Uruguayan Carnival featured performances on stages called Candombe, Murga, and Tablados. The carnival had evolved into a dance parade where different comparsas played drums and danced to music during the "Desfile Inaugural del Carnaval" and Llamadas parade. Amanda played a jovial character while Maria was her dance partner. They enjoyed the festival immensely.

They sampled asado and local delicacies while locals celebrated watching their hero Maria take part in their cultural activities. This exemplified Localization using the Prime Directive from New-Way Ideology—moral and ethical guidelines prohibiting outsiders from infringing on local cultural and linguistic sensibilities.

Maria emphasized that there were many ways to preserve local norms, including cultural and linguistic traditions, beliefs, customs, and values. Implementation steps according to New-Way Ideology included language translation, cultural reference adoption, constant feedback, and continuous refinement. It was essentially a framework for respecting local cultures in all their diversity with dignity and respect.

"In all this New-Way Governance transformation," Maria stressed, "one must never lose sight of local cultural and social treasures. Without preserving local heritage, people won't support the governance system." Vish understood this aspect of localism and gave localization a significant role in New-Way Governance.

Amanda and Matheus, with their teams, designed localization policies and frameworks for data collection during New-Way implementation in Uruguay. They spent months in Montevideo in a temporary office building near the World Trade Center, meeting with local people and political leaders to understand cultural nuances.

Amanda and Matheus debated local societal issues with local representatives, particularly those affecting South America. After extensive study of Vish's concepts, they concluded these ideas were more necessary now than ever, showing the path to a bright future of equality, respect, dignity, freedom, and progress.

When asked hypothetically, "Would you choose preserving local culture or choose progress that diminishes local culture?" Maria stated, "Vish's Ideology would choose preserving local culture with dignity and respect, if that represents the locals' informed choice."

Matheus recalled conversations with local people, marveling at how well the population's thinking aligned with their leaders about progressive concepts. Uruguay was already among the world's best countries for free speech and progressive thinking. This generally tolerant mindset made implementing New-Way Ideology significantly easier.

Maria was instrumental in bringing these changes to fruition in Uruguay. The Uruguayan population adored her, treating her as their spiritual guide. Symbolically, they even erected a statue in her honor. Maria and her teams ensured that policies and principles—including the Dichotomy of Politics and Administration, Autonomy of Administration, Decentralization of Governance, Localization using Prime Directive, Just-in-Time Economy, and Globalization of Safety and Security—were meticulously implemented at the field level.

A vast, redundant sensor network was deployed to collect raw data and transfer it to central computers for processing and analysis. Sensors were positioned everywhere—above ground, underground, in air and space, and underwater—creating ubiquitous coverage that could withstand catastrophic failures by using fault-tolerant mechanisms. The sensor networks monitored every aspect of human life: weather parameters, infrastructure quality (roads, buildings, water bodies), safety of life, quality of living and much more. Daily data collection reached petabytes at each community level.

The data management complied with the highest security standards through New-Way Cryptographic architecture. It also featured efficient storage, secure transmission, and rapid analysis capabilities. Yet it stayed completely transparent, allowing changes and feedback from communities. Citizens continuously accessed information according to their LifeScore through protected, interactive data management and feedback mechanisms. The last step in data management involved analyzing data that is replete with raw realities and ratified by community representatives. This ensured human essence wasn't lost in autonomous budgetary allocations and decision-making process.

Amanda explained implementation details of local autonomous administration at the convention, drawing on her expertise in sensor technologies and computer systems.

An audience member raised her hand. "I have a question."

"Yes, please go ahead," Amanda replied.

Elizabeth from Colombia asked about autonomous administration: "What if there are errors in data collection? What if sensors are hacked, become erratic, or simply go offline?"

"Excellent questions, thank you for asking," Amanda responded. "Data collection operates with complete independence from external influence. The collected data reflects ground reality in quantified form through Adit's specialized algorithms that manage collection, storage, analysis and transmit. All processes adhere to strict government safety and security regulations. The gathered information transferred securely to failsafe, hacker-proof central servers. Community members can access data based on their identity credentials, with the ability to make necessary changes according to their privileges. Once the data is validated and finalized, it feeds into the budgetary allocation system for various management and administrative tasks during implementation."

This process represented an everyday continuous cycle: collecting data, capturing feedback, transferring to central servers, analyzing and preparing metrics, and finally making the data actionable for decision-making.

"There are many questions about data processes, especially since politician aspect removed from the traditional equation," Amanda continued, "Data collection, transmission, analysis, and dissemination remain completely transparent to citizens and open to questioning. Local administrators and councils field questions, rectify issues, and provide clarifications. Data points are fundamental to New-Way Governance, with their data quality mirroring reality at nearly 100 percent accuracy. Confidentiality, Integrity, Availability, and Honesty are the process cornerstones."

Uruguay implemented New-Way Ideologies holistically, including Autonomous Administration, Localization of Governance, Dichotomy of Administration, Just-in-Time Economy, and Inter-State Diplomacy. Political leaders dealt only with Inter-State aspects concerning international communities and countries. The definition of New-Way living in practice was nearly perfected, and it was nowhere better exemplified than in Uruguay. The hardworking population now had direction and guidance from Vish's human-centric ideology.

People worked for decent living and worked harder to earn luxurious living of their choosing. No hard work meant no luxury. The New-Way framework supported the “One for All and All for One" ethos. People found jobs they enjoyed or that suited them, sharing material resources for common causes, thereby increasing their LifeScores.

The emphasis on local cultures and societies resulted in contentment about self-respect and dignity among local populations. Because of New-Way Ideology's inherent "*helping not hurting*" culture, peace prevailed in New-Way countries. As Maria emphasized, "*New-Way ideology measured progress by human well-being.*"

Globalization for Safety and Security

Social and economic safety and security challenges were varied and complex, reflecting the inherently interconnected nature of global societies and economies. These challenges include poverty and inequality, conflict and violence, climate change, migration and displacement, and cross-border corruption. Addressing them requires comprehensive and integrated approaches, including effective policies and programs, international cooperation, collaboration between local and national governments and international organizations, and investment in education, health, and social protection.

Security was a topic of complexity with global scale and impact. Challenges and impacts could reach from local to global levels and vice versa. Global-local, or '*Glocal,*' interdependence has become a key element in addressing post-modern local safety and global security challenges.

In today's interconnected world, Safety and Security challenges were becoming increasingly complex. Developments such as globalization and the spread of networked, hyper-connected technologies presented new safety and security challenges affecting local, regional, national, and international societies. These challenges dramatically increased in complexity and scale.

Globalization has both positive and negative impacts on safety and security. Positively, globalization increased interconnectivity, making it easier to share information and coordinate efforts addressing global security threats such as terrorism, cybercrime, and pandemics. It led to greater cooperation between countries and international organizations. Negatively, globalization increased the likelihood of infectious disease spreading faster and made it easier for criminals to operate across borders and jurisdictions. Furthermore, globalization contributed to cross-border corruption and economic and political imbalances, potentially contributing to social unrest and conflict.

Adam and Eva initially worried that the old guard wouldn't relinquish status quo partisan and selfish politics. Hailing from Uruguay, where New-Way ideology was strongest among following countries, they were initially skeptical about acceptance of New-Way Safety and Security concepts among the general population. However, everyone recognized that currently neither administration nor politicians had adequately addressed people's safety and security needs. Much of this malaise was attributed to rising protectionism and nationalism.

Adam and Eva were from San Antonio, Uruguay—a peaceful town about an hour north of capital Montevideo. Though small, the town was resilient and reflected life in complete freedom: no fear of robbery, no fear of exploitation, and a population living with respect and dignity.

Few would believe or understand that their safety and security depended on local economies as well as macro-level connections to the entire planet. Maria brought forth

New-Way ideas about basic human safety needs, their interconnection to global well-being, and how local well-being could be secured.

Maria believed that stronger constituents create stronger communities and vice versa. However, benefits from outside the community were never available if communities remained sealed off from the outside world. For benefits such as the ability to acquire knowledge for the benefit of local societies, people must be attuned to the global contexts. Maria noted that this balance was precisely what New-Way Ideology achieved—a near-perfect blend of localization and globalization.

Maria understood that Safety and Security issues were formidable and challenging, capable of making or breaking a community's peaceful existence and threatening individuals from reaching their full potential. Local issues were relatively easily faced, addressed, and mitigated because they were visible, felt, and easily understood. These issues were resolved locally with local knowledge and resources. However, issues resulting from indirect and external forces—macro economy, social influences, rapid advancements, and climatic changes—were more formidable and needed addressing at higher levels through interconnecting local entities with global entities.

Adam and Eva, along with New-Way Ideology volunteers from Uruguay, attended training sessions presented by Maria. These were well-balanced with theory and simulation games for real-life implementation exercises. Simulation games were designed by Adit and enhanced by other Core members in their respective areas of expertise. For the first time, attendees learned how safety and security were multi-layered for every citizen and were definable and tunable according to individual and community needs.

Eva gave Adam a book titled "New-Way Theories 101," about implementing New-Way theories and concepts in real-world scenarios. This book was authored by the New-Way Core Group. Adam read it at the first opportunity and felt relieved learning about New-Way concepts, complexities and implementations. When he re-read *the Book,* everything made sense. Adam recognized that the world desperately needed to shift toward selfless approaches focused on human well-being. The next morning, Adam thanked Eva: "Eva, thank you so much for the book, it made me clearly understand what Vish was proposing for the new world order!"

Adam and Eva were delighted as Uruguay's population experienced the best safety and security of their lives—better than under any earlier governments and regimes in recorded history. People witnessed their societies change drastically before their eyes while cultural richness and its nuances remained preserved.

When Maria first visited this town, she instituted several local governing groups with Adam and Eva as members of local governing committees. These local committees align well with national Safety and Security committees, focusing on integrating local economies and societies with national levels.

The currency was digital and global. NeWay Coin was used in all transactions across New-Way countries, whether domestic or international. This made monetary and fiscal policies transparent and corruption-free. Since these countries adopted the global cryptocurrency, economies and trade became truly open and interconnected. Transactions became seamless using digital ledgers with advanced blockchain technologies, supported by Adit and his team's state-of-the-art secure transaction framework.

Global challenges—including public conscience crises, immigration and refugee issues, natural disasters, warfare, cybercrime, terrorism, pandemics, and environmental catastrophes—had become increasingly urgent and immediate for every person, regardless of location or nationality. New-Way Safety and Security framework proved to be highly relevant in the 22nd century, specifically designed to address these interconnected global threats. Through the New-Way governance paradigm that prioritized honesty and selflessness while maintaining clear humanitarian goals, these challenges were effectively confronted and resolved.

Inter-State Politics and Space Colonies

Inter-State and Space Colony politics represented a governance thread of New-Way Ideologies, referring to political relations and diplomacy between different nations including space colonies. The UN New-Way Councils—that included outer space entities—provided guidance and advice to member countries for Climate, Economy, Education, Healthcare, Research, Safety, Security, and Peace. All six New-Way countries had their own space colonies.

Some space colonies became self-sufficient and declared independence from Earth while pledging allegiance to their chosen earthen countries. Inter-state and space colony politics presented complex and challenging issues, given space colonies' unique nature and potential for geopolitical tensions extending to space. Key challenges included jurisdiction and sovereignty, resource allocation, international cooperation, space environment regulation, and security and defense. These challenges underscored the importance of international cooperation and developing effective governance and political structures ensuring inter-state-space colony success and sustainability.

New-Way Ideology core members working on various committees helped write the UN New-Way Constitution, providing guiding principles for countries to conduct themselves equitably. Resources from various countries were pooled and distributed to countries in need, ensuring that all resources were shared. This system ensured that countries lacking certain resources would receive them judiciously. This global fair allocation was possible only through the interconnected nature of the countries according to UN New-Way policies.

Research and development for various initiatives, creating medicines and treatments, new materials, climate preservation, zero-gravity or micro-gravity production in space-based labs, Quantum Information Processing (QIP) facilities, next-generation internetworking, newer transportation techniques, and heavy capital investment projects—were fully funded and monitored by UN New-Way Councils. The UN set up facilities for these projects globally in collaboration with participating countries. The benefits of these endeavors were distributed directly to the populations of member countries based on their needs, as determined by their LifeScore metrics.

Leaders from these UN councils convened meetings and conducted workshops for members' benefit. The sole guiding principle for UN New-Way Organizations was catering to people's benefits across national border lines—globalization and localization in simultaneous play. The sole purpose of UN bodies was protecting, preserving, and progressing population well-being by creating wealth and distributing this wealth equitably.

Wars—implicit or explicit—between nations were prohibited. Various built-in provisions prevented member countries from working against each other. Nations now participated cooperatively and truly globally. For New-Way countries, there was no option to remain outside the New-Way UN. Every country was included, each providing funding pro-rated based on population and other metrics.

Autonomous Budgetary Allocation

The underlying assumption for community budgetary allocations was that funds were always available for any project, as resources were provided by the respective councils. Monetary and fiscal policies abandoned zero-sum financing treatment. All resources belonged to national governments, and people received what they needed and wanted through CHEFS and LifeScores framework.

Goods and services were created, produced, and added to national grids following Just-in-Time Equinomy. Derivatives trading was banned. Profiteering was banned. Taxation was banned. Insurance was banned. Traditional buying and selling of resources were banned because the market-based economy inherently introduced inequalities and profit mongering. Market economies provided scope for reckless entrepreneurial and consumer behavior detrimental to general populations and ecology.

The New-Way marketplace functioned as an inventory map of goods and services, allocated according to each person's LifeScore. Transactions used Quantum Blockchain technology to prevent corruption and to scale to any imaginable level. This mechanism applied to both cross-border and outer-space transactions. Goods and services were made available using extensive master lists, with production and distribution made strictly based on needs. This economic model eliminated profit and loss. Unused, unallocated, or unclaimed items—a rare occurrence—returned to available inventory lists. Master lists guided decisions on when and what goods to start or stop producing and served as the basis for distribution. This ensured that resources weren't wasted on unwanted items.

"The aim of New-Way Governance," Maria explained, "was not perfection or ideal society but rather focused on progressing well-being and removing hurdles in its way. Hence, it's not a utopian society possible only in imagination. New-Way Ideology focuses on reducing inequality while creating wealth and reaching well-being for humanity. This was the challenge—a challenge of motivation, innovation, wealth creation and fair distribution—that Capitalism, Communism and Socialism faced but couldn't answer. New-Way Ideology avoided this pitfall by implementing CHEFS and LifeScore Governance."

Interstate and space colony politics often involved conflicts over resources, territory, power, and trade. These conflicts took many forms, from diplomatic bargaining to economic sanctions to protectionism. The Core Team designed an Inter-State and Space Colony political system based on strong foundations of mutual respect, trust, and cooperation. This required shared commitment to democratic values, rule of law, and human rights, plus effective mechanisms for dispute resolution and conflict management from participating countries.

There was a huge global interest in learning about New-Way Ideologies and their implementation details from participating countries. The Core group conducted conferences with a full attendance of people listening to ideologies.

Maria and the Core Team formed committees, each based on member countries. She also set up working groups attached to each continental group. These groups were tasked with addressing doubts and satisfying the curiosity of those wanting to learn more about new-way ideologies. This included reforms in governance, preserving cultural aspects, reducing inequalities, changing monetary and fiscal systems, and enhancing socially responsible behaviors.

Maria chose delegation and dispersion techniques for managing these demanding tasks. Because of the communication revolution, implementing an idea became easier if people welcomed the ideas. New-Way Ideology was such a philosophy—people worldwide trusted its intent and immediacy, welcoming it overwhelmingly.

Core group members each developed detailed plans covering major aspects of life. Key issues included Climate, Equitability, Safety and Security, International Cooperation, Brotherhood, Healthcare, Education, Wealth Creation, and well-being. CHEFS and LifeScore were at New-Way Ideology's heart, and this philosophy enabled people to work harder.

Inter-State politics was the mechanism for member countries to understand their strengths and weaknesses. It helped compare with other countries and develop plans to share excesses from each country with others. equitably—the essence of Equinomics. This wasn't viewed as a utopian concept but rather as a necessity for progressively living better.

Diverse and Inclusive Social Fabric

Life is an eternal struggle to balance inclusivity and exclusivity, both essential aspects of existence. Many spend their lives in dissatisfaction and frustration, searching for purpose and meaning. Vish believed that the true meaning of life lies in fully experiencing existence, echoing philosopher *Iddo Landau's* well-known assertion that we already possess everything necessary for a meaningful life. Vish's followers affirmed the belief that it's unnecessary to search for life's meaning, purpose for living, or destiny in life concept. This is because life is ephemeral, and one should strive to live and experience it fully with compassion.

The New-Way Core Team knew that building diverse and inclusive social fabric required efforts and participation from all community members. This included promoting equality, understanding, tolerance, and actively working to remove barriers preventing certain people from fully participating in society. According to Maria, diverse and inclusive social fabric refers to society composed of individuals with divergent backgrounds, perspectives, beliefs, cultures, races, ethnicities, and sexual orientations. In New-Way communities, everyone had equal opportunities to participate and contribute.

Maria spearheaded the New-Way Social Fabric movement, as envisaged by Vish, through relentless efforts to bring equitability and fairness. Significant changes in global political systems have heralded the emergence of new power centers worldwide. The United States, China, and European Union had lost much of their old-world hegemony with the onset of new power centers: Uruguay leading South American Union, Nepal leading South Asian Union, New Zealand leading Pacific Union, Slovenia leading European Union, Canada leading North American Union, and Namibia leading African Union. Technological advancements, demographic shifts, and environmental challenges resulted in emergence of local governance and participatory democracies. Citizen initiatives, local referendums, and other forms of direct and participatory democracies were enabled by following New-Way political, administrative systems, social concepts, and economic systems.

Maria ensured decentralization of power in New-Way countries, with citizens having real-time say in decision-making processes. New-Way political systems allowed networked democracies to emerge, where citizens were decision-makers using advanced technology. This system involved networks of local, regional, and global decision-making bodies interconnected through digital platforms, enabling citizens to participate in democratic processes on more direct and meaningful levels. Participation in the democratic processes was mandatory and rewarded with LifeScores.

Within New-Way democracies, individuals took part directly in decisions on all matters impacting their lives, guided by the principle of community consensus. It enabled more nuanced and localized governance approaches, where decisions were made based on specific communities' needs and priorities rather than top-down, one-size-fits-all policies. To make this system work, a triumvirate of advanced technological infrastructures was deployed: secure remote voting systems; decentralized, redundant databases; and AI analytics tools that surpassed human intelligence—yet operated within strict guardrails—to enable real-time citizen participation.

In addition to direct democracies, other political systems appeared following New-Way tenets, prioritizing sustainability and equality, such as circular economy-based systems or common minimum social programs. These systems prioritized the planet's long-term health and well-being for all its inhabitants rather than short-term gains for a few. With Equinomics, the New-Way economic system, resources would be managed and distributed to minimize waste and maximize reuse, reducing human activity's adverse environmental impact.

The UN New-Way political and governance system was called "Global Governance", a cooperation system between various governments and civil organizations to address 21st century challenges. Global governance was a complex network of institutions and organizations working together globally to achieve common goals. This global governance system facilitated international cooperation on issues such as climate change, public health, ecology, and economic development. It involved various actors, including national governments, international organizations, non-governmental organizations (NGOs), and other multinational organizations.

At the heart of global governance were institutions like the United Nations, World Bank, and World Health Organization. These organizations provided platforms for countries to coordinate efforts on global issues. However, global governance wasn't limited to formal institutions. It also involved wide-ranging informal networks and partnerships between governments, civil society groups, and private sector actors. These networks allowed information exchange, best practices sharing, and coordination on specific issues.

One of global governance's key strengths was its ability to bring together diverse stakeholders and perspectives. By involving wide-ranging actors, including grassroots level participants, global governance aimed to ensure policies and programs were informed of various perspectives and tailored to local and global contexts.

At the same time, global governance faced significant challenges, including issues of accountability, legitimacy, and the disproportionate power held by certain actors—particularly multinational organizations and wealthy nations. In response, greater emphasis was placed on good governance principles such as transparency, accountability, and inclusive participation. Efforts intensified to involve civil society organizations and ensure that the voices of marginalized groups were represented in decision-making processes. A key innovation in this context was LifeScore—a metric designed to recognize and reward positive human participation.

***

Equinomics

Economics of Equity

Vish introduced the concept of *Equinomics*—an equitable economic system that served as the foundation for shared prosperity. This New-Way Ideology organically emerged as a replacement for legacy economic systems that had proven inadequate in delivering both equity and sustainability.

Vish drew sharp comparisons between New-Way Equinomics and traditional economics. While conventional economics merely addressed production, distribution, and consumption, it failed to provide an answer to the crucial question: how do societies fairly distribute their precious resources? This monumental failure triggered a cascade of disasters—rampant overconsumption, systemic inequality, environmental devastation, and endless wars. In place of sustained human progress, it left only a gaping void of missed potential. New-Way Equinomics emerged as the transformative solution, wielding four powerful tools: fair distribution, controls on waste, uncompromising environmental protection, efforts to invent newer methods and sustainable progress by intelligent resource allocation.

The key Equinomics policy framework items included:

Inclusive Economic Growth: Focusing on policies that foster fair economic development.

Innovation Priority: Prioritizing R&D in clean energy, resource-efficient technologies, and circular economy models

Well-being Metrics: Moving beyond GDP to comprehensive measures like the Human Development Index and Genuine Progress Indicator

Universal Basic Income (UBI): Implementing UBI to support the CHEFS model.

Natural Resources Management: Sustainably managing natural resources to prevent degradation and depletion.

Untapped domain utilization: New domains prioritized for budget allocations for R&D, manufacturing, mining, and colonization.

LifeScore Integration: Using the LifeScore model to foster responsibility, motivation, and innovation.

Adit and Maria explored ways to align sustainable resource utilization with universal well-being, understanding that creating such systems posed intricate challenges to economic and social structures. They posited, "While pursuing equitable outcomes, how can we ensure sustainable resource usage to support long-term innovation and progressive outcomes?"

Adit and Maria, along with the Core Team, deliberated on implementing New-Way ideology of Equinomics for sustainable and progressive economics. Their analysis explored potential avenues and considered both established economic theories and newer innovative paradigms. They concluded that New-Way Ideology was perfectly positioned for implementation in 22nd century like never before. This unprecedented transformation arose from a unique historical convergence—the ***'Great Social Chasm'*** occurring, as at the end of 21st century, alongside the breakthrough emergence of triumvirate of advanced technologies.

The core team cautioned that implementing this radical, untested approach called Equinomics would face immense challenges. Status quo proponents and vested interests benefiting from current resource allocation systems would oppose vehemently. Adit noted that various existing 21st century frameworks could provide insights and guidance. For example, the global Sustainable Development Goals (SDG) addressed three dimensions of sustainability—economic, social, and environmental. The Circular Economy concept was crucial—an economic model aimed at minimizing waste while safeguarding the environment, contrasting with the traditional linear economy that maximized output without environmental regard. A circular economy could also contribute to social well-being by reducing inequalities and enhancing health and education. However, SDG and Circular Economy faced challenges and limitations, including GDP focus, rebound effects, infrastructure and institutional lock-in, lack of consumer awareness and behavior change, and potential trade-offs with other environmental and social objectives.

In New-Way Equinomics, economies of scale were integrated with Just-in-Time and Just-for-Need production to optimize resource usage. By maintaining a precise 1:1 production-to-consumption (P2C) ratio, the system minimized wastage and ensured efficiency in resource allocation. Consumers accessed the Universal Master Product Catalogue to place orders, while producers adhered strictly to demand-driven production (DDP), manufacturing and delivering only what was requested. This approach emphasized managing aggregate demand to ensure equilibrium through a lean production model that eliminated excess inventory.

The Core Team recognized criticisms that New-Way Equinomics amounted to glorified catalogue management that would create oppressive bureaucracy. The Core Team responded by creating autonomous catalogue systems that matched production to *just* demands while keeping control over consumption patterns, made possible with the advent of triumvirate of advanced technologies.

The New-Way production and consumption controls added an innovative regulatory layer, where consumer purchases were governed by their LifeScores, and production was strictly limited to consumer orders. This framework ensured Pareto-efficient resource allocation, as supply and demand were perfectly matched, leaving no room for surplus production or excess consumption. By cutting overproduction—a common issue in traditional supply-driven models—and avoiding waste associated with unchecked consumerism, this Equinomics model achieved a sustainable and balanced economic system.

Adit emphasized that the Core Team believed in New-Way Equinomic policies that addressed legacy economic issues and set out to implement sustainable policies for comprehensive benefits.

Production of Goods and Services

Vish proposed "economic and social homeostasis" a balanced state of economic and social well-being. New-Way Equinomics strived to balance needs and wants by deploying CHEFS and LifeScore methods in governance. He believed technological advancements could allow this balanced well-being to be achieved in the 22nd century.

Market economy and its futile equilibrium between supply and demand were the bane of modern economics that only resulted in consolidated inequality and disequilibrium. It neither cared for the poor's needs nor tempered the rich's wants. The Core group understood this was Vish's motivation to find a true balance between wants and needs and seek proper production to cater to the *just* demands.

In modern economies, the share of national income going to wages and salaries decreased while share of capital owners increased. Poverty remained as a widespread problem. Equinomics policies were designed to address this untenable 21st century economic state.

Adit was in London to deliver a lecture at the London School of Economics later that week. The day before his famed "New-Way Equinomics 101" class, he met with like-minded professors and students from local universities. According to New-Way Ideology, Adit explained, society's success should be judged by how effectively it improved the material, social, and spiritual well-being of every citizen. So, Vish's Equinomics ensured every citizen received an equitable share of material benefits. He emphasized that New-Way Equinomics focused on holistic progress for the entire population.

The group concurred that wars, climate change, pandemics, biodiversity loss, global inequality, resource depletion, and environmental degradation posed existential threats to humanity. Addressing these challenges requires urgent action using innovative technological advances in clean energy, new materials, genomics, and resource conservation.

"For too long, we measured progress through crude aggregates that disguised reality behind rising income statistics," Adit continued. "What appeared as economic growth was actually a widening chasm between rich and poor—one that kept expanding. This happened because our financial and monetary systems remained fundamentally inequitable, driven by short-term thinking, nationalism, selfish governance, and protectionist policies. The well-being of entire populations was simply ignored."

Professor Gwen from Cambridge raised her hand. "But Adit, didn't GDP growth at least indicate some level of progress? Surely rising incomes meant something?"

"That's exactly the illusion I'm talking about," Adit replied. "GDP growth often meant wealth concentration, not distribution. We now understand that genuine fulfillment transcends personal income. True prosperity depends on safety and security, physical and mental health, and quality public services that deliver the essential components of CHEFS."

A student from the back called out, "Can you give us a concrete example of how this inequality actually hurts the economic performance?"

Adit nodded. "Certainly. There are numerous examples within every society. The *Great Social Chasm* stood for the profound inequalities in both material and mental well-being that divide humanity. Twenty-first century economic systems were built on the unethical exploitation of natural resources—practices that were neither fair nor sustainable. This systematic plunder has triggered climate change and ecological collapse, which now pose catastrophic threats to economies and societies worldwide." He paused, scanning the audience. "Empirical evidence shows that unequal societies are economically poorer than more-equal societies. In this sense, fairness and prosperity go hand in hand. Well-being surveys consistently show that more equal societies are also those where life satisfaction and happiness are highest."

Dr. William, an economist from LSE, leaned forward. "That's a compelling argument, but how do you convince policymakers who are still focused on traditional growth metrics?"

"By showing them the cost of ignoring these realities," Adit responded with conviction, "the data is overwhelming to show that inequality doesn't just hurt the poor; it drags down entire national economies."

Reducing inequality could boost economic growth and significantly affect both social and individual well-being.

Studies across developed countries in the 21st century showed strong correlations between inequality and various social harms, including higher rates of mental and physical illness, crime, lower levels of social trust, low educational attainment, and low social mobility. These effects resulted in environmental unsustainability, rising inequality, monopoly corporate power, politics and money interplay, indiscriminate market derivatives, and rampant monetization. Each arose from dysfunctional structural features of 21st-century modern economies—features that were brazenly selfish and inherently profit-driven.

Adit knew that factors of production—inputs that create goods and services—needed tempering and conservation. New-Way governments carefully designated these scarce resources to cater to CHEFS programs while creating wealth according to New-Way Wealth Metrics, ably supported by the LifeScore mechanism. Adit emphasized that optimum production and discrete consumption were at the crux of Vish's envisioned New-Way Equinomics.

New-Way Equinomics 101

The "New-Way Equinomics 101" class, taught by Adit at the London School of Economics, was a remarkable academic event held on a large football field on campus. It drew over 10,000 in-person attendees, with many more participating remotely. The open venue facilitated a vast audience while creating an engaging environment. The school digitally broadcasted the event over television, radio, 6G digital, holographic, and AR/VR formats in real-time. Adit commanded immense respect among educationists, economists, researchers, and technologists for his demonstrated expertise in traditional economics, advanced technologies, and in revolutionary New-Way Equinomics.

Adit's class highlighted New-Way Equinomy that benefits humanity at large. He lucidly explained implementation details that had shown results in the current six New-Way countries. Speaking from the podium, Adit explained "New-Way Production and

Consumption" as direct, one-to-one alignment between individual needs and production factors while considering national and global priorities. This approach represented a "just production" system where goods and services were created and supplied precisely to meet actual needs while addressing inefficiencies and mismatches in production and distribution.

The production-distribution-consumption lifecycle was regulated by New-Way Governance. Unlike traditional market economies' demand and supply paradigm, this new model prioritized producing and supplying goods and services in just-in-time fashion. It matched the provisions of CHEFS program *needs* while responding to *wants* shaped by individual LifeScores. Determination of who qualified as deserved was guided by individuals' sustenance CHEFS needs and personal LifeScores.

In New-Way Equinomics context, newer paradigms evolved: Just-in-Time production, LifeScore-based consumption, ethical resource utilization, and producer-to-consumer (P2C) distribution models. This was facilitated by centralized master product catalogs enabled by 22nd century technological advancements. Various master catalogs were created with participation from governments, producers, and consumers. Managing catalogs was a real-time process with real-time updates and relevant safeguards.

Consumers placed orders from Universal Product Master Catalogues maintained by governments. New-Way nations implemented singular, centralized Master Catalogues for various product classes and categories, making them easily accessible to both consumers and producers. Producers cross-checked consumer orders using Product Master Catalogue items before manufacturing. Producers were responsible for transportation and delivery directly to consumers, eliminating intermediary roles. Digital ledgers, powered by blockchain technology, securely and transparently recorded transactions in an open and reliable manner. Traditional supply chain mechanisms, characterized by intermediaries such as hoarders, wholesalers, retailers, commission agents, and brokers, became obsolete.

The 21st century economies, even with state intervention as in Mixed or Hybrid models, could not offer fair wealth distribution and universal population benefits. They distributed wealth in unbalanced fashion while those welfare measures only perpetuated inequalities, resulting in more misery for the poor. The minority—powerful and rich—garnered the most benefits. For instance, from the 2040s to 2090s, a staggering ninety percent of the population collectively held less wealth than the richest one percent, hence the label '*Great Social Chasm*'.

Adit was captivated by Vish's suggestions for minimizing wastage of time and resources. He embraced the idea of checking excesses of production and consumption in goods and services. Vish's dictum '*Spend just enough resources*' was the production and consumption mantra. To develop an optimum economic system, one needed to determine and deploy efficient ways to produce just enough goods and services while ethically conserving resources. Vish called this *Equinomy, the optimum equitable economy.*

Adit understood that living by these ideals required using the least number of resources to produce what was truly needed by those who needed it most. Since resources were limited and often scarce, new ways to use them more efficiently were essential. Technologies of the 22nd century made it possible to discover new natural elements and create advanced materials. These and other breakthroughs came through the combined power of triumvirate of key technologies. The New-Way initiatives led to major innovations—such as mining resources from asteroids and other celestial bodies and developing new synthetic materials in zero-gravity space laboratories.

Vish gave us a clarion call to "*Realize, Rise, Redirect, Rebel, and Rule*"—in the face of inequality and injustice. Adit recognized that revolution follows an eternal cycle—the ***5R***s that mark humanity's path to liberation. ***R****ealize*-the inequality. ***R****ise*-in rebellion. ***R****edirect*-toward justice. ***R****ebel*-against oppression. ***R****ule*-with wisdom. These developments are not products of chaos, but the predictable outcome of unchecked greed and collapse of ethics among the privileged elite. New-Way Equinomics was designed not merely to acknowledge these ***5R***s, but to harness their revolutionary power for humanity's transformation.

The change in Uruguay leading to New-Way adoption was easiest compared to other countries such as Namibia, New Zealand, Slovenia, Sri Lanka, and the UAE.

Distribution of Goods and Services

The core goal of New-Way Equinomics was to ensure fair access to goods, services, and opportunities for all individuals. Vish's fundamental belief was that every person deserved equal opportunities simply by virtue of being alive.

"Despite centuries of philosophical struggle," Adit declared, "social justice and economic equality remained impossible dreams for majority through the late 21st century. Countless thinkers had tried and failed." His voice strengthened. "But Vish achieved what others could not. His New-Way Ideology didn't just theorize—it integrated every aspect of human society: governance, administration, economics, politics, sociology, and spirituality. For the first time in history, we had a comprehensive system dedicated solely to crushing inequality and unleashing human potential."

Retailers vanished as producers shifted to a make-to-need model. Traditional intermediaries, such as wholesalers and retailers, became redundant. This system eliminated practices like hoarding, price gouging, artificial shortages, supply control mechanisms, and unfair speculation.

Manufactured goods shipped straight to consumers' destinations. Producers' Warehouses became central to goods and services distribution. These warehouses kept products only for direct just-in-time transportation to consumers, most efficiently.

The most economical and environmentally friendly transportation mode, known as *Graviport* (gravity-assisted transportation), operates using rail or cable cars or vacuum tubes over air or land or water. This system leveraged gravity to move containers along tubes or rails or cables between towers of varying heights, enabling natural gravitational slides along slopes.

For example: In the case of vacuum pipes, a 20-degree slope would produce 3.35 m/s^2 acceleration due to gravity alone, and a package of any weight would reach its destination in about 25 seconds over a one-kilometer distance.

Loading and unloading were energy-efficient too, utilizing counterweights to lift or lower loads without requiring additional energy. New-Way Equinomics ushered in new and efficient transportation modes for people and products. Transportation on cables, levitating automobiles, and vacuum-enclosed highways were commonplace. Charging-in-transit became a game changer in transportation. New-Way Graviport transportation leveraged airways and waterways in ways not dreamed of in the 21st century, reducing carbon footprint while achieving highest energy efficiency.

Powered mechanisms such as propellers or jet-powered containers could be employed on Graviport infrastructure for even faster transportation. Drones were integrated to assist in lifting and shifting containers, making them lighter and easier to move along rails or cables. Additionally, a range of other technologies—including autonomous vehicles, satellite internet, hoverboards, jetpacks, flying-ships, and drones—were seamlessly deployed in daily life, ensuring efficient and versatile transportation solutions.

Adit's Quantum Information Processing (QIP) solutions revolutionized cryptography, artificial intelligence, supply chain management, blockchain, robotic automation, transforming production, transportation industries, and other areas. Technologies like quantum analytics, Internet of Things, digital ledgers, and smart contracts now govern transactions, accounting, and record-keeping. Integration of these advanced tools enabled efficient supply chain management, secure transactions, and keeping transparent records, ensuring fairness and accountability in New-Way Equinomics and governance.

Consumption of Goods and Services

An individual's state of well-being is not determined by the amount of material consumption.

The concept of CHEFS coupled with LifeScores ensured that consumption was regulated and aligned with healthy and sustainable practices. Individuals could only order what their LifeScores allowed, preventing overconsumption and promoting responsible resource utilization. New-Way Ideology's success extended beyond economics and justice; it fostered social justice, economic equality, and spirituality. By providing fair access to goods, services, and opportunities, the system addressed long-standing inequality issues and unfair resource distribution.

John Maynard Keynes' Consumption Policy tied income and employment. Consumption (C) is a function of disposable income (Yd), expressed as: **C = a + bY** [where 'a' is autonomous consumption (consumption when income is zero) and 'b' is the marginal propensity to consume (MPC)]. It did not address disproportionate consumption or destabilizing effects on resources. In New-Way ideology, one could consume beyond CHEFS entitlements only when their LifeScore permitted. Wants, as opposed to needs, were classified as luxuries and could be only obtained or bought by using personal LifeScores.

This addressed both disproportionate consumption and destabilizing effects on limited resources.

The rampant consumerism that dominated through the end of the 21st century wreaked devastating consequences: systematic resource abuse, toxic waste dumped from wealthy nations into poorer ones, obscene extravagance amid crushing poverty, and waste production that reached truly farcical proportions. The entire foundation of legacy production and consumption economics demanded radical transformation.

Adit and the Core Team developed a revolutionary but implementable Production and Consumption Policy. Adit ensured that personal freedom and privacy were not infringed upon, following Vish's ideologies that freedom, self-respect and dignity were the highest qualities of human living.

Respective country leaders managed Consumption levels according to New-Way Equinomics, where production, distribution, and consumption were fair in local and global humanitarian contexts. In the New-Way paradigm, consumption was viewed through sustainability and equitability lenses. The traditional economic model, driven by capitalistic ideals, fostered overconsumption and wastefulness culture, particularly among affluent society segments. This excessive consumerism led to finite resource depletion, environmental degradation, and a widening gap between haves and have-nots, all of which resulted in unrest and wars.

Recognizing such practices resulted in unsustainability, New-Way Equinomics advocated for more mindful and responsible consumption approaches. The overarching principle was - consuming only what was necessary for supporting a healthy and dignified quality of life, avoiding frivolous, extravagant, or vanity consumption.

At the heart of New-Way Equinomics lays a revolutionary concept: LifeScore as the cornerstone of economic activity. This innovative metric functioned as both a wealth indicator and the primary determinant of resource allocation and consumption rights. Through LifeScore-based distribution, New-Way Equinomics sought to create unprecedented equity—guaranteeing that every person's essential needs and desires were fulfilled while preventing the wasteful excess that had plagued earlier systems. This framework embodied a profound understanding: genuine well-being transcended material accumulation, requiring instead the delicate harmony of physical, social, emotional, psychological, and spiritual fulfillment.

New-Way Consumption Policy

The Consumption Policy, developed by Adit and the Core Team, served as a framework for regulating consumption at national and international levels. One key principle of the Consumption Policy was contextualizing consumption from a local and global perspective. Rather than viewing consumption through narrow, personalized, and local lenses alone, New-Way Equinomics advocated for global approaches that considered global well-being.

To implement this system effectively, New-Way Equinomics relied on New-Way Governance. Consumption patterns were closely checked to identify waste or excessive consumption instances, with proper measures taken to rectify such instances. This oversight level was not intended to infringe upon personal freedom or privacy but rather to ensure resources were used responsibly in ways that promoted everyone's well-being.

Stringent measures were in place to discourage and penalize excessive consumption, while incentives were provided for responsible and sustainable practices. For example, individuals who consistently adhered to sustainable consumption patterns might be rewarded with higher LifeScores, granting them access to additional resources or opportunities!

Furthermore, the Consumption Policy promoted efficient resource use by encouraging practices such as recycling, reusing, and repurposing. This not only reduced waste but also minimized strain on finite resources, contributing to the sustainability of the global ecosystem. It also enforced ethical consumption where disproportionate consumption, at others' expense, was discouraged by penalizing or disincentivizing using LifeScore assignment mechanisms.

By adopting New-Way Equinomics and its Consumption Policy, New-Way countries moved away from old economic models that focused on irresponsible growth, overproduction, and overconsumption. Instead, it embraced more balanced and ethical ways of using resources and improving overall well-being. By fostering mindful consumption culture, respect for human dignity, and global collaboration, this new economic paradigm had potential to pave the way for a sustainable and equitable world for generations to come.

New-Way Commerce and Trade

Vish realized that business conduct evolved with the times from barter systems to colonization, to commerce, to tariffs, and then to free trade, aided by evolving political and economic systems of their times and places. Most legacy economic systems were based on profit generation and the motive that trickle-down effects would cater to population needs and wants. But it was clear that none of these methods succeeded in well-being even at the end of the 21st century. Besides, most economic systems openly professed betterment of the rich at the expense of poor.

Vish recognized that a simplistic produce-and-supply-to-need system would quickly result in a centralized bureaucratic system that would be inefficient, corrupt, and defeat purposes of innovation and motivation for population's progressive well-being. So, Vish proposed a new method of exchanging goods and services. This commerce and trade would be innovative, global, resource-conserving, and aware of environmental balance. Vish introduced a Universal Value system for exchanged goods and an exchange method using universal currency—a Digital Token. To this effect, the Core Team introduced the NeWay Crypto token, a truly federated digital currency. This covered the entire gamut of resource transactions including production, storage, distribution, and consumption.

New-Way Trade was fundamental economic activity involving goods and services exchange between two or more parties—inside-border or cross-border parties—at an agreed Universal Value. In contrast, New-Way Commerce encompassed all activities facilitating the trade between producer and consumer, including distribution and logistics.

Adit noted that the 21st-century capitalism model prioritized wealth creation by rewarding innovators and entrepreneurs, serving as a powerful catalyst for rapid economic growth, albeit unbalanced and unethical. This system enabled unprecedented riches for those smart and sharp enough to seize and exploit opportunities to their advantage. In that era, abilities of intelligence and exploitation became the most valued traits, elevating individuals and organizations to immense power and influence. Consequently, power became concentrated in ultra-wealthy, exploitative, and affluent hands. However, this rapid lopsided progress, propelled by advancing technologies and resourceful elites, came at fairness' cost, lacking equity and perpetuating systems where wealth and power were increasingly unevenly distributed.

The 21st century commerce and trade with various international agreements became exploitative, with sole aim of self-benefit for participating individuals, groups, or countries. To address this exploitation, the New-Way World Society—an apex global organization—was formed based on New-Way Ideology. It was set up with the help of New-Way Countries, much like the old-world UN but without its flaws or weaknesses. Operating within global context frameworks as its guiding principles, this Apex organization provided direction to member countries across five critical domains: Equinomics, Governance, Justice, Research and Development, Education, Healthcare, and Spirituality.

Profiteering was not allowed. Profiteering—the practice of making unreasonable profit, often only possible through unethical or unfair means—had been subject to various regulations and bans throughout history. New-Way Governments and regulatory bodies implemented measures to stop profiteering. These measures are aimed at protecting consumers from value gouging and ensuring fair economic practices.

Enforcement encompassed comprehensive monitoring of production and consumption patterns, strategic management of LifeScore allocations, and swift imposition of penalties on violators. While the specific implementation of these measures varied by jurisdiction and local context, the fundamental goal remained constant: preventing exploitation while guaranteeing equitable access to essential goods and services.

New-Way Ideology presented a compelling alternative to traditional economic, political, and social systems—one that prioritized the well-being of all humans and sought to set up harmonious balance between individual progress and collective prosperity. While the path ahead was undoubtedly challenging, it offered a glimmer of hope for a fair and just world.

New-Way Fiscal Policy

In his "New-Way Equinomics 101" lecture, Adit provided a succinct overview of the world's major economic systems. The global economic landscape had been molded by diverse approaches, each carrying distinct philosophies about resource allocation, production, and distribution. Throughout the 21st century, two models reigned supreme: capitalism and mixed economies, which together shaped the financial destinies of most nations across the globe.

Capitalistic economies, the most popular, were characterized by free-market systems where production means were primarily controlled by private entities and individuals. In this framework, supply and demand laws governed goods and services production and pricing, with minimal government intervention. Capitalism proponents argued this system fostered innovation, efficiency, and economic growth by allowing market forces to operate freely. This system worked on the assumption that it also took care of general population prosperity with trickle-down effects.

Monetary policy, as implemented by 21st century independent central banks, played crucial roles in capitalistic societies. These institutions aimed to influence money and credit quantity within economies through various mechanisms, such as adjusting interest rates and controlling money supply. By manipulating these levers, central banks could influence economic activity, combat inflation, and promote stable growth.

Fiscal policy, complementing monetary policy, referred to government decisions regarding taxation and spending. By adjusting tax rates and implementing spending programs, governments could directly impact aggregate demand, stimulate economic activity, and address socioeconomic imbalances. During economic downturns, governments might increase spending or reduce taxes to boost consumer demand and spur economic recovery. Conversely, during excessive inflation or overheating times, governments might tighten fiscal policies to cool economies.

Adit presented empirical evidence showing how monetary and fiscal policy mechanisms generated cyclical economic fluctuations that consistently benefited an elite minority, who accumulated greater wealth through each downturn and recovery—exemplifying what was termed as "insider economy" dynamics.

While pure capitalism and command economies represented opposing extremes, mixed economies struck middle ground by combining elements of both systems. In mixed economies, private sectors coexisted with government intervention and regulation. This hybrid model aims to harness free markets' efficiency and innovation while addressing market failures and promoting social welfare through government policies and programs. Mixed economy definition characterized economic systems where both private markets and governments exercised control over production factors. This hybrid approach constituted the dominant economic paradigm globally, seeking equilibrium between unfettered market forces and targeted governmental intervention to address both market inefficiencies and broader societal imperatives.

Adit showed that the mixed economy served as a sophisticated deception mechanism, allowing the powerful and wealthy to maintain control while creating the false impression among the disadvantaged that governments were genuinely advocating for their interests.

To assess 21st century market economy performance and health, economists and policymakers closely watched key economic indicators. Inflation, measuring the cost of goods and services over time, served as critical price stability and purchasing power indicators. High inflation rates could erode consumer confidence and hinder economic growth, while deflation could lead to stagnation and reduced investment.

Employment levels, measuring individual incomes, reflected population proportions engaged in productive work and capable of earning, spending, and investing. Robust labor markets with low unemployment rates were generally viewed as positive economic vitality signs.

Housing markets, where rising property prices could stimulate bank lending and economic growth, offered valuable insights into consumer confidence and overall economic health.

Consumer spending, a driving force in consumption-based societies, was closely watched as it directly impacted on economic growth and business profitability.

The confidence Index, although intangible, played pivotal roles in shaping economic trends, as it underpinned consumer and business sentiment, influencing investment decisions and overall economic activity.

Adit challenged the assumption that legacy economic indicators genuinely helped the needy and deserved. He argued that these metrics functioned as deceptive tools representing apparent improvements in aggregate data while systematically obscuring individual hardships and disparities.

Adit pointed out that Vish introduced, as part of his Equinomics framework, a revolutionary concept: the New-Way Commerce and Trade System. This system would demand that New-Way governments adopt highly autonomous and centrally coordinated and planned strategies for resource allocation and service delivery, all the while staying responsive to citizens' evolving needs. Complexities of human behavior regarding work, exchange, and incentivization in such systems were addressed with CHEFS and LifeScore by deploying the 22nd century triumvirate of advanced technologies.

Cryptology

This New-Way Equinomics recognized limitations and shortcomings of prevalent 21st century economic, fiscal, and monetary systems. It retooled and fortified fiscal systems while completely removing the monetary system and replacing it with a combination of LifeScore metrics and NeWay Cryptocurrency. Trade tax was eliminated, thereby eradicating cross-border exploitation associated with various tax policies. Individual tax was eliminated to eradicate indiscriminate taxation, which resulted in tax evasion, black money, parallel economy, lowering taxes for the rich, etc. Instead, New-Way governments maintained the New-Way Well-being Index (NWI). This index was used by countries to request or supply resources. This innovative framework aimed to address economic inequity, instability, and inefficiency issues by introducing revolutionary value-backed cryptocurrency, the NeWay Crypto token. LifeScore could be converted into Cryptoken at rates set by respective governments. Every transaction was now conducted using NeWay Crypto tokens. This mechanism indirectly ensured mapping transactions with actions.

Although traditional cryptocurrencies provided the benefits of decentralization and transparency, they were fundamentally flawed for practical application—lacking identifiable intrinsic value, plagued by extreme price volatility, and burdened with unnecessary complexity that made them impractical for legitimate business operations or widespread usage. Vish's NeWay Crypto token mechanisms aimed to fix these issues by tying its value to a variety of real-world assets. These assets included precious metals, commodities, real estate, gaming cards, and other tangible holdings, with a special emphasis on LifeScores. The goal was to turn LifeScore metrics into a commodity. This approach of backing the token with real assets was designed to give the NeWay cryptocurrency an intrinsic value that is based on tangible economic and social fundamentals. The intention was to create the stability and reliability needed for the cryptocurrency to be widely adopted as a trusted medium of exchange.

Privacy and transparency were central tenets of NeWay Crypto token architecture. While ensuring transaction and user identity anonymity, the system aimed to support high transparency degrees through immutable and publicly accessible ledgers. This duality sought to balance individual privacy and institutional accountability, fostering system trust and confidence.

Leveraging Quantum cryptographic techniques, the New-Way Trade System aimed to safeguard users' holdings from unauthorized access or manipulation. Furthermore, it envisioned facilitating seamless and instantaneous cross-border transfers without traditional financial intermediary constraints, enabling truly global and borderless transactions.

Additionally, Equinomics offered open crypto account services, ending entry barriers and fostering financial inclusion for individuals and communities traditionally underserved by conventional banking systems. To ensure the system's long-term viability and integrity, Vish's vision included setting up robust legal frameworks to govern the New-Way Trade System. Clear guidelines, regulations, and protections for all stakeholders were envisioned, creating stable and transparent environments for the adoption and implementation of this innovative economic paradigm.

Although ambitious and challenging, Vish's core economic ideas inspired new thinking in digital finance and alternative economic models. As the world continued grappling with economic disparities, environmental concerns, the rapid pace of technological advancement, innovative approaches like New-Way Equinomics offered possible paths toward fairer, more sustainable, and people-centered economic systems, hence named Equinomics.

Adit and Maria, along with the Core Team, ensured that New-Way Equinomics remained tied to humanity's well-being in broader contexts.

New-Way Applied Technology

Adit was a visionary leader whose brilliance spanned technology and economics. His expertise in fields like Internet of Things (IoT), Quantum Information Processing (QIP), and Artificial Super Intelligence (ASI) was unmatched as demonstrated by numerous high-profile patents he had held.

His groundbreaking contributions left lasting impacts on both economy and society. Adit developed blockchain solutions that transformed sectors such as business, healthcare, and education, streamlining processes and revolutionizing exchanges.

Determined to address long-standing computing security issues, Adit used Quantum Information Processing (QIP) power to create hacker-proof cryptography systems and unassailable blockchain mechanisms. This innovation resolved critical vulnerabilities, enabling secure communications, transactions, and data storage. By fostering digital trust, it paved the way for exploring new transactional applications previously considered too risky.

Adit used the triumvirate of advanced technologies—Nuclear Fusion Energy, Artificial Super Intelligence, and Quantum Information Processing—to develop and deploy many New-Way methods. He developed Quantum Security Tokens that played key roles in securing IoT sensor networks and data collection process. In New-Way countries, billions of sensors were deployed, collecting real-time data and transmitting them to fusion-powered central quantum servers. These servers provided advanced storage, analysis, reporting, and feedback, enabling never-before-seen data-driven decisions on massive scales. By combining IoT, FPE, ASI and QIP, Adit laid groundwork for intelligent systems that could monitor, analyze, and optimize processes autonomously, boosting efficiency in real-time across industries.

Beyond technology, Adit and his core team designed comprehensive frameworks for economic transactions. These frameworks supported interactions at every level—local, national, international, and space colonies. They prioritized transparency and accountability, ensuring all transactions were auditable and trustworthy.

The applied nature of Adit's scientific inventions was instrumental in their successful real-life implementations across myriad domains. The New-Way Digital Token, Digital Ledger, Blockchain, and Smart Contract were seamlessly integrated within the revolutionary New-Way Transactions framework, ushering in a new era of open, secure, efficient, and transparent transactions.

Through his groundbreaking work, Adit, ably supported by the core team, transformed the technological and economic landscapes, reshaping how we perceive and interact with these vital fields. His innovative solutions not only enhanced computational efficiencies but also ushered in a new era of secure transactions, robust data analysis, and unprecedented opportunities for growth and development across various sectors.

One of Adit's genius hallmarks was his ability to bridge gaps between theoretical concepts and practical implementations, ensuring innovative scientific advancements were not confined to laboratories but were actively translated into real-world applications benefiting societies. His work empowered individuals, businesses, and governments alike, providing them with tools and frameworks necessary to navigate digital age complexities with confidence and trust.

In a world where technology was inextricably intertwined with all other sectors, Adit's contributions became indispensable, shaping the very fabric of how we live, work, and interact with one another.

***

Ethical and Moral Progression

Participatory social choices impact societies.

The dynamics of social, cultural, and ethical progression form a complex and reciprocal system influenced by cultural nuances, historical contexts, collective human experiences, technological advancements, and spiritual depth. Understanding these dynamics is crucial for fostering a fair and harmonious society.

An ideal relationship functions as a partnership built on mutual responsibility toward one another and the broader community. This perspective positively impacts both personal and community well-being by requiring mutual respect, empathy, and shared values and goals. Strong social connections, for instance, can alleviate stress and enhance resilience.

Lea asserted that New-Way Choices inherently provided simultaneous personal and societal benefits. This ideology placed relationships at the heart of human progress, introducing comprehensive frameworks for volunteerism, purpose-driven partnerships such as marriage, and social activism. The LifeScore system supported these relationships by allocating higher scores for healthy and positive life choices, including marriage, community participation, and civic responsibility.

Under the New-Way ideology, the nuclear family is redefined as a voluntary and legally recognized agreement between two consenting individuals who mutually commit to shared caregiving responsibilities and the upbringing of children—biological or adopted—through to the children's legal age of majority. Vish advocated for ending inheritance, arguing that it fostered greed in grantors and complacency in heirs. Instead, the New-Way LifeScore metric became the primary currency of value, rewarding individuals for meaningful contributions to relationships and society during their lifetime.

"LifeScore can be used for personal, family, or institutional benefit while alive, and all accruals will be lost at the individual's death," Lea declared, reinforcing the focus on living purposefully and impactfully. The system requires all donations of personal LifeScore credits to be strictly voluntary, well-documented, and devoid of coercion.

Lea highlighted how LifeScore incentivized actions such as strengthening family relationships, building community, and promoting collective well-being. The New-Way HappyChoice relationship, which carried higher LifeScore weights, encouraged the formation of families and social units, fostering collaboration and mutual growth.

In her influential book, "Theory of Social Everything," Lea addressed contemporary challenges like informed consent, evolving gender roles, and technology's impact on courtship. She explored how New-Way relationships adapted to future trends, from 22nd century interpersonal relationships to reproductive technology advancements to shifting legal frameworks, ensuring balance between tradition and innovation.

"Association and companionship are the cornerstones of evolutionary relationships," Lea stated. Drawing from Vish's teachings, she emphasized the importance of understanding the historical, cultural, and ethical dimensions of relationships. By fostering inclusive and respectful personal relationships with social responsibility, Lea believed humanity could achieve greater social harmony and universal well-being in the 22nd century.

Social Service Providers

In New-Way Ideology, social service providers earned higher LifeScore values and hence higher respect. They helped individuals, families, and communities across many areas. These areas include Learning, Research, Healthcare, Entrepreneurship, Policing, and Administration. Each area had specific values and weightages in the LifeScore formula. For example, life-saving innovations and binding healthy relationships earned higher scores.

Lea and the Core Team transformed social services under New-Way Ideology. They focused on well-being, spirituality, and collective growth. Teachers, scientists, healthcare workers, and community leaders received higher LifeScores. This recognized their important contributions to society.

Grassroots volunteerism became essential to community development. A master catalog lists community projects for all skill levels, making it easy for anyone to choose from and contribute to those projects. While participants earned generous rewards for their volunteer work, the LifeScore incentive system encouraged widespread participation and strengthened social bonds throughout society.

"Actions helping communities earn exponential value. Harmful ones get logarithmic deductions," Lea explained. The LifeScore formula adapted to diverse cultures and geographies. It held people accountable for their actions.

New-Way ideologies promoted mindfulness, self-awareness, and sustainability. They value community building and environmental protection. Society's well-being mattered as much as individual success. Social service organizations, nonprofits, and community centers embraced these principles. They worked to help marginalized groups and promote social justice. The system encouraged volunteering from an early age. Altruistic actions received higher scores.

People at every level receive help from this system. In New Zealand, Akenehi and Amelia offered free scuba diving and swimming lessons. Their volunteer work earned them high LifeScores. They gained free facilities and resources, access and community recognition. With their impressive scores, they planned to buy a beach house and yacht. Their service brought both personal rewards and community benefits.

New-Way Justice System

Fundamental human rights ought to be protected and enforced.

Vish defined Universal Justice as "fairness and equity bound by fundamental human rights." Thus, evolved New-Way Justice System dictum as, "Human rights enable dignity and respect to flourish". All actions fall under the scrutiny of the Justice System," Vish stated.

Fundamental human rights were reinforced through the New-Way Ideology as governed by the CHEFS and LifeScore framework. For example, CHEFS provide for:

Clothing - Basic attire and protection
Healthcare - Medical care and wellness services
Education - Learning and skill development
Food - Nutritional sustenance
Shelter - Safe housing and protection

These rights are guaranteed at the subsistence level through government funding, with the possibility to earn more through the LifeScore system based on one's hard work and contributions to society. The system ensures fundamental rights are not privileges but inalienable rights of citizens for just being born and alive.

LifeScore defined the Human Actions Framework to highlight relevance and consequences of active or passive participation in society.

The New-Way Justice System also emphasizes these fundamental principles that are protected by its governance:

Justice - Fair treatment and equal access to justice systems
Freedom - Personal freedom balanced with collective responsibility.
Dignity and Respect - Everyone deserves inherent dignity regardless of wealth or status.

Equal Opportunities - Equal access to participate and contribute to society.

The New-Way Judicial System functioned as the supreme authority above all branches of governance. Unlike 21st-century justice systems bound within constitutional mandates, New-Way Justice system established itself as a non-negotiable and immutable apex entity, effectively replacing the traditional constitution. It governed politics, enforcement, administration, and press—making every action accountable to justice.

Vish revolutionized the justice system by focusing on human well-being rather than punishment. "Stop crime by stopping the causal contexts and behaviors," he declared. Research proved that the certainty of being caught—not severity of punishment—deterred crime most effectively.

Justice meant reconciliation, not retribution. Lea explained, "New-Way justice enforcement prioritizes rehabilitation with spiritual guidance over penitence." The system ensured equal access to wealth, opportunities, and privileges for all. Any infringement on individual freedom or harm to others—mental, physical, direct, or indirect—construed as a crime. The approach was innovative and compassionate:

Minor infractions received understanding and second chances.

Mid-level offenses led to spiritual centers for guided counseling and growth.

Serious crimes faced appropriately severe penalty including capital punishments.

Three simple questions determined justice:

1. Have your actions harmed anyone directly or indirectly?
2. Have you infringed on someone else's fundamental rights?
3. Have you acted with greed and selfishness?

"These questions reveal whether someone crossed ethical lines," Lea stated.

The Justice System operated through community-based justice councils that rolled up from local to national levels. The Justices were highly educated, trained across disciplines, and committed to ethics and fairness. Justices on the councils made up of appointed as well as elected. Mexico in the mid-21st century offered a unique precedent—the direct election of justices by the people. Grace, Lea and Core Team helped set up these hybrid councils in Namibia, New Zealand, Slovenia, Sri Lanka, Uruguay, and UAE.

Spiritual Centers replaced traditional prisons for most offenders. These centers focused on values and enlightenment through community service and teachings. Remarkably, work in these centers earned LifeScore points—the same rewards given for positive contributions elsewhere. This penance system motivated rehabilitation: once offenders accumulated enough points, they could choose their own work assignments or even get released to the mainstream life.

"The entire mechanism encourages freedom and choice rather than state-assigned punishment," Lea explained. The goal was "*Lagom*" consequence with blended individual choice—a Swedish concept meaning "just right"—neither too harsh nor too lenient.

Technology enhanced justice delivery. The Core group's Judicial Technology Architecture enabled instant participation by all stakeholders—monitors, counselors, judges, prosecutors, defenders, and citizens. The system quickly identified perpetrators and served appropriate responses.

LifeScore deductions served as the primary deterrent. Negative scores indicated need for correction. Capital punishment existed only for extreme, unrepentant criminals—a tiny fraction of offenders. Most received opportunities for redemption through community service.

Grace observed, "Addressing greed and selfishness prevents hurt. When people want more than they need, they likely infringe on others' rights. Only spiritualism can check this behavior."

The Justice Council's mandate was clear: preserve and progress humanity with dignity. As Vish defined it, "Justice governs all political, economic, and social systems. It is a humane ideology—not an individual supremacy."

Lea and the Core Team published the "New-Way Justice System Collective" as the definitive guide. Their vision: a world where ethically driven representatives oversee justice, creating harmonious communities through equality and freedom. This wasn't just a reform, it was a transformation. Justice became proactive, not reactive. Preventive, not punitive. Spiritual, not merely legal.

Here's a detailed exploration of what New-Way Governance would look like:

Leadership Structure: The Justice Council would establish leadership committees that included community leaders and scholarly professionals. Each member would bring in unique perspectives and expertise. The areas they covered were economic, political, and social systems with the goal of preserving and sustaining progressive humanity. Governance and Policies would ensure: Human Rights and Equality, Environmental Protection, Cultural Sensitivity, Compliance and controls.

A world thus governed by Justice Councils would strive to embody primary ideals of justice. With their collective abilities and ethical compasses, the council(s) would guide in addressing systemic challenges much ignored in the past.

For Vish, Human Dharma was pluralistic and layered, referring to individual actions taken in service of the well-being of all humanity. It could be understood as a fusion of Greek Deontology, Hindu Dharma, African Ubuntu, and the Consequentialism of 18th- and 19th-century philosophers like Jeremy Bentham and John Stuart Mill—reinterpreted through the lens of contemporary 22nd century social contexts.

Lea posited that *Sanātana Dharma*, as understood within Hindu philosophy, could be understood as a fusion of religion and spirituality. She argued while Sanatana Dharma traditionally encompasses both religious practices and spiritual principles, these components can be analytically separated.

In her analysis, the spiritual dimension—characterized by introspection, the pursuit of wisdom, cultivation of tolerance, and mindful consideration of consequences—represents the universal and humanistic core of Sanatana Dharma. When abstracted from its institutional religious context (organized belief systems, rituals, and sectarian boundaries), these spiritual principles constitute a philosophical framework truly conducive to universal human flourishing rather than merely to the well-being of respective religious adherents.

Lea further developed a comprehensive taxonomy of justice, identifying multiple intersecting dimensions:

Distributive Justice: concerning the fair allocation of resources and opportunities.

Social Justice: addressing systemic inequalities and power imbalances.

Restorative Justice: focusing on healing and reconciliation.

Procedural Justice: ensuring fairness in processes and decision-making.

Retributive Justice: dealing with proportionate responses to wrongdoing.

Environmental Justice: recognizing ecological rights and intergenerational equity.

She acknowledged that conceptions of justice are inherently shaped by cultural and philosophical traditions, leading to legitimate pluralism in their interpretation and application. Nevertheless, she maintained that justice represented a universal and free human aspiration—an ongoing endeavor aimed at constructing societies that embody fairness, equality, and respect for human dignity. This involves developing institutions and systems that promote equity, safeguard individual rights, and provide mechanisms for the fair resolution of conflicts.

Diverse cultures and legal systems emphasize certain principles or approaches to justice, such as retribution, restoration, or distributive justice. Philosophical perspectives, ranging from utilitarianism to deontology, also shape justice interpretations and guide decision-making processes.

While specific manifestations and interpretations of justice might differ, the underlying aim remained consistent: to create a society where all individuals had equal access to opportunities, were treated fairly, and had their rights safeguarded. The New-Way Judicial System was further developed by Lea and the Core Team to be adopted by New-Way Governance. The ideologies were based on Vish's pronouncements on justice, punishment, and the consequences of human actions. Lea appreciated Vish's idea of human life's precious nature. "*Human life is the most precious and one should value it by actions that only preserve it,*" Vish stated.

Lea believed in Vish's views of the System of Justice. The system should be such that, whichever way one looked at it or understood it, it should bring benefits to humanity. The system must provide win-win paradigms. When law violators received pertinent punishment and law adherents received encouraging rewards, that was a win-win for society.

Samepage – New-Way Communication

Language serves as both an instrument of expression and a medium of communication while acquiring cultural connotations. The elegance, richness, and profound meanings conveyed by language depend heavily on how it is utilized. Various forms of language exist, including spoken, written, visual, and even performative acts. Ultimately, what matters most is the effective transmission of intended meaning at a given time, place and context.

Lea devoted considerable time and effort to studying languages and linguistics. She observed that in current societies, superstrate and substrate languages coexisted, often creating tension due to entrenched beliefs in one language's superiority over another, a notion that persisted well into the late 21st century despite its inherent unfairness.

Lea noted that throughout history, certain cultures faced subjugation by groups claiming linguistic superiority. The use of language as a tool to oppress population segments, still observed today, presents a troubling parallel to other evolutionary changes in human society. Linguistic theories suggest that language naturally evolves to meet its community's needs. According to *muted group theory*, dominant groups shaped language to keep their dominance, often marginalizing less powerful groups' experiences. Lea argued that when language became a vehicle for expressing superiority or denigrating others, it was crucial to relinquish such condescension.

In response to these issues, Vish proposed a language designed to reduce interpersonal and intercultural differences. He envisioned a medium that facilitated the shared socio-cultural communication platforms, emphasizing content over structure, emotion over format, and knowledge preservation. This approach ensured clear expression of intent while minimizing misunderstandings. Thus evolved the language *Samepage*—a New-Way communication medium rooted in New-Way ideology, prevalent social contexts, and 22nd century technology.

Samepage language lent itself remarkably well to advanced language technologies, aligning seamlessly with interconnected linguistic systems such as phonology, morphology, syntax, semantics, pragmatics, lexicon, discourse, orthography, sociolinguistics, and cognitive frameworks. Each element contributed to how humans communicated meaning, formed ideas, and used language in various social contexts.

Lea collaborated with Adit and other Core Team members to formalize this New-Way language's transport mechanisms. Technological advancements introduced many communication options, such as holographic transmission, brain-machine interfaces, brain-to-brain communications, augmented and virtual reality, body-implanted chips, etc.

Under Lea's leadership, the Core Team championed and evangelized the New-Way language, Samepage, which became a de facto standard in New-Way countries and showed promise as a universal language. Samepage integrated words and expressions from multitudes of languages and cultures. It featured systems of phonemes, combinatorial graphemes, and digraphs, enabling true representation of about 55,000 current English language words with unique meanings, making it easier to learn than the world's most popular language, English. Samepage achieved one-to-one correspondence between graphemes and phonemes, representing ideal phonemic orthography.

"Adoption of the Samepage language will take time, but its potential is vast to serve us well into the 22nd century and beyond," Lea emphasized.

Vish created the foundation for Samepage language, with the Core Team expanding upon it in line with New-Way Ideology. As a language, Samepage showed cognizance of languages' history and modern communication needs. Lea highlighted that learning

Samepage language was straightforward. The language was rich but subtle in vocabulary, pronunciation, and grammar, allowing for wide-ranging thoughts, ideas, emotions, expressions, and intentions, while also being well-suited for digitization and quick adoption.

Adit noted that Samepage structure facilitated a near real-time bi-directional translation with other languages using acoustic codec devices developed by himself and Folapr. Dictionaries of Samepage had sprung up and been established, with translations available in various languages. Given its roots in technological advancements, instant translations were possible through modern communication methods like brain-machine links and chip implants. Communicating with anyone in any language was effortless with Samepage, especially when integrated with the latest related technologies.

New-Way countries had adopted Samepage as additional official language alongside local languages. The results were phenomenal, and the reason was that Samepage as a language lent itself extremely well to electronic transmission and natural human expression simultaneously.

"We have successfully implemented Samepage across various digital, print, holo, and spoken formats," Lea stated.

Lea compiled a comprehensive guide on Samepage language principles, emphasizing its role in fostering a just society. The key principles included:

Respect and Inclusion:

Use language that honors all backgrounds and identities.

Avoid terms that stereotype, demean, or exclude any group.

Stay aware of unconscious biases encoded in language around race, gender, and class.

Challenge Oppression:

Question "neutral" terms that hide discrimination.

Examine linguistic conventions that reinforce inequality.

Amplify marginalized voices overlooked by mainstream narratives.

Build Bridges:

Foster constructive dialogue between different communities and beliefs

Find shared values across ideological divides.

Create space for public discussion of ethical dilemmas and social issues.

Promote Truth and Dignity:

Frame communication to affirm fundamental human rights.

Counter propaganda and misinformation that divides communities.

Recognize power dynamics in who controls communication platforms.

Center Social Responsibility:

Prioritize truth and understanding in all messages.

Use compelling stories to connect people with justice causes.

Make social responsibility the foundation of communication.

This framework ensured Samepage language to unite rather than divide, heal rather than harm, and elevate rather than diminish human dignity.

Each of these elements contributed to how humans communicated meaning, formed ideas, expressed emotions, and used language in various social contexts and interactions. "Communication that humanizes 'the other,' fosters common ground, addresses exclusion, and enables civic discourse as essential in the pursuit of a just and equitable society," Vish asserted.

Language and communication were essential tools for creating a just society—a 'Vasudhaiva Kutumbakam,' as the Sanskrit phrase beautifully expresses: 'The world is one family.' When used positively, they built understanding, promoted dialogue, and challenged injustice. However, language could also create division and inequality, spreading hate speech, promoting stereotypes, and silencing marginalized voices.

Lea gave specific examples of how language and communication could promote Just society:

Inclusive language: Use terms that did not exclude or marginalize people from diverse backgrounds. For example, replace "mankind" with "humanity" and "fireman" with "firefighter."

Respectful communication: Engage in discourse free from insults, name-calling, and other forms of disrespect, even when disagreeing.

Storytelling: Leverage stories' power to build understanding and promote dialogue, helping people see the world from different perspectives and understand others' experiences.

Activism: Use action to bring about social change, challenging injustice and creating more just society through positive activism.

Culture Directive of Inclusiveness

Every culture possesses inherent value and dignity.

Lea drew inspiration from Star Trek's Prime Directive to shape Vish's Culture Directive—a principle that every culture and individual deserves respect and dignity, demanding inclusive recognition. She encouraged people to become multilingual while adopting Samepage as a universal communication medium.

Collaborating with her team, Lea developed comprehensive guidelines to preserve local cultures while ensuring the directive remained accommodative, accessible, and inclusive. The Culture Directive established that all people deserve respect and dignity, regardless of differences. It recognized everyone's right to live meaningful lives and contribute to society. Tolerance and patience became the major virtues.

The Culture Directive of Inclusiveness had implications for how we should interact with each other. It placed tolerance and patience as one of the highest virtues. *First*, it meant that we should be mindful of our own biases and prejudices and consciously overcome those, and that we should strive to treat everyone with fairness and equality. When people were treated fairly and equally, they were less likely to be discriminated against or marginalized. It helped promote social cohesion and harmony. *Second*, it meant that we should be open to learning about other cultures and perspectives, and that we should be willing to challenge our own assumptions. When people felt respected and valued, they were more likely to be productive and positive members of society. *Third*, it meant that we should be supportive of those who were different from us, and that we should work to create a more inclusive society. It helped foster innovation and creativity.

When people from diverse backgrounds come together, they enrich each other as they share ideas and perspectives, which can lead to new and innovative solutions to problems. Key Elements of such an effort would make up:

- Equal access and opportunities.
- Diversity and representation.
- Social justice and equity.
- Empathy and understanding.
- Collaboration and participation.
- Continuous learning and improvement.

Living the Directive of Inclusiveness demands ongoing commitment, learning new perspectives, and unlearning biases. As Lea emphasized, New-Way thinking recognizes that while no one is perfect and everyone differs, we can amalgamate the best of humanity to build stronger communities.

The Culture Directive serves as both a reminder and a call to action: build societies that value and uphold all individual's rights and dignities.

Dimensions of an Equitable and Fair Society

Society was a complex system that could be analyzed and understood through various dimensions. Vish chose to propose judicial, economic, political, and social frameworks as extremely important dimensions of society for their practical and progressive purposes. Spiritual dimension was all encompassing and covered all aspects of the organizations.

Judicial Dimension: The judicial dimension of society was primarily tasked to measure and judge every action or inaction of the population on a human well-being scale.

It encompassed the beliefs, values, customs, and traditions shared by its members but checked against usefulness or hurtfulness to society at large. The goal was to achieve equity and fairness.

Economic Dimension: The economic dimension of society focused on the production, distribution, and consumption of goods and services. It examined factors such as economic systems, wealth distribution, and natural resources. This dimension explored economic structures and processes that shaped livelihoods, opportunities, and living standards within society. The goal was to achieve economic equity.

Political Dimension: The political dimension of society encompassed systems, institutions, and processes through which amity was achieved, and international affairs were managed. It involved studying governance structures, political ideologies, cultural heritage, and citizen participation. This dimension examined political power and authority distribution and its impact on societal dynamics and individual rights. The goal was to achieve political equity and administrative independence.

Social Dimension: The social dimension of society focused on patterns of social relationships, norms, values, and institutions that shaped social interactions and behavior. It included aspects such as family structures, education systems, healthcare, social stratification, and cultural practices. This dimension explored the ways in which individuals and groups interacted, formed social bonds, and created shared meanings within society. The goal was to achieve social equity.

Spiritual Dimension: The spiritual dimension of society was all encompassing and focused on tying together all aspects of living.

These dimensions were interrelated and influenced one another, shaping the overall fabric of society and humanity at large. Creating an equitable society involves addressing various dimensions to ensure equal opportunities, rights, and outcomes.

These aspects were interconnected and mutually reinforcing. Building a fair society requires comprehensive efforts across the five fundamental dimensions, the primal constructs, tackling systemic barriers, to promote inclusivity, and to ensure justice and equal opportunities for all individuals, irrespective of their backgrounds or circumstances.

***

Healthcare and Education

The state of the population is measured by the quality of its health and education.

Equal access to New-Way CHEFS services, which covered Healthcare and Learning, was the aim of New-Way Ideology. To achieve this goal the CHEFS Monitors mechanism was instituted to enforce accessibility, quality, technology integration, workforce enablement, research and development, resource allocation, and public engagement.

Healthcare - Fundamental Human Right

In the grand design of New-Way Ideology, healthcare emerged as a keystone—an essential pillar among the sustenance-level necessities encapsulated in the acronym CHEFS (Clothing, *Healthcare*, Education, Food, Shelter).

Sparq and Grace led healthcare initiatives, ably guided by the Core Team, creating a comprehensive Healthcare Policy that seamlessly integrated healthcare into New-Way Governance. Healthcare was elevated beyond mere service to become a cornerstone of societal progress. Sparq and Grace championed this cause with unwavering commitment, understanding that population well-being formed the foundation for all societal advancement.

The Core Team was aware of the disparities in accessibility to these services as at the end of the 21st century. The below quick statistics based on incomes, as obtained from UN WHO, reveal a complex global health landscape with significant but substantial challenges remaining, particularly in achieving equitable access to healthcare:

Health Indicator	High-Income	Low-Income
Life Expectancy	85+ years	About 65 years
Infant Mortality	< 5/1,000	> 35/1,000
Health Spend (per capita)	About $8,000	< $100
Access to Safe Surgery	> 90%	< 35%

Thus evolved the CHEFS program which decoupled the disparities when accessing these basic services.

The New-Way Health paradigm positioned healthcare providers as champions of well-being. The system operated under directed volunteerism with directed focus, where every service manifested collective will and commitment to society's well-being. This comprehensive Healthcare ecosystem comprised of:

Medical Professionals

General practitioners to specialized experts (cardiologists, neurologists, etc.)

Frontline custodians of community health

Patient Care Staff

Nursing personnel

Integral components of healthcare delivery

Health Facilities

Hospitals, clinics, and R&D organizations

Operating under directed-volunteerism principles.

The New-Way model transcended traditional boundaries. Government assumed health stewardship, ensuring healthcare was an inalienable right, not a privilege. This egalitarian approach fostered humanitarian care focused on proactive health preservation rather than merely treating ailments.

New-Way governments set up various higher medical education institutions. These institutions served multiple purposes:

Innovation Beacons

Pushing medical knowledge boundaries

Fostering groundbreaking research

Collaboration Hubs

Connecting researchers, clinicians, and industry partners

Creating ecosystems for breakthrough development

Transition Centers

Converting discoveries into real-world applications

From gene therapies to brain-computer interfaces

The global perspective extended beyond national boundaries. Institutions were strategically placed based on local governance needs, preventing duplication and optimizing resources—honoring Vish's principle against resource waste.

The dictum "Health is a fundamental human need" became the guiding principle. New-Way Ideology recognized health as intrinsic as essential as a heartbeat.

Government assumed the role of benevolent guardian, offering comprehensive healthcare services:

- Primary and ambulatory care
- Urgent and intensive care
- Rehabilitation services
- Prescription medicine
- Diagnostic care

Every aspect remained 100 percent free to citizens, challenging conventional narratives where financial barriers dictated access.

Accountability Through LifeScores

While advocating free healthcare, the system promoted personal responsibility. Sparq emphasized healthy lifestyles to manage costs effectively. Grace acknowledged that genetics, aging, and environmental factors still influence health despite healthy living.

The accountability system worked as follows:

- Those neglecting healthy practices used personal LifeScores for such health costs.
- When illness was beyond personal control, governments fully covered those costs.
- Human conditions never became discriminatory factors such as age, disease, etc.

In this CHEFS method, technology and health integration was achieved through:

- Directed medicines.
- Human-machine interfaces.
- Genetic treatments.

- Epidemiological controls.
- Prosthetic enhancements.

Yet Vish's emphasis on spiritual methods remained paramount. Kirl wove spiritual aspects into daily life—meditation, nature connection, social interactions, and physical activities became pathways to health, peace, and stability.

"Healthcare service is not merely a catalog of offerings; it's a testament to the realized comprehensive care," Sparq declared.

The New-Way Public Foundation

At the heart of this philanthropic movement stood the New-Way Public Foundation, overseen by the Core Team. This influential trust focused on activities directly promoting New-Way Governance and ideologies. The foundation managed diverse portfolios including:

- Traditional and New-Way funds.
- Legacy currencies and NeWay Cryptocurrency.
- The revolutionary federated LifeScore Bank.

Through USD one trillion in donations by the year 2100, the foundation fueled comprehensive reforms in Sri Lanka, New Zealand, Slovenia, Namibia, Uruguay, and the UAE.

The Core Team's approach challenged conventional philanthropy by:

- Addressing root cause of societal inequalities.
- Empowering communities for long-term self-sustenance.
- Investing in education and skill development.

- Fostering individual autonomy and potential.
- Adapting solutions to local values and practices.

Their efforts embodied the principle "All-for-one and One-for-all." It inspired the Core Team members to contribute their personal wealth, and LifeScores to the collective well-being.

New-Way associates including Dr. YoloMunk, Krishna, and AJ actively engaged with institutions and the public, imparting wisdom through fieldwork and direct communications. Their collective efforts proved that through compassion, vision, and shared commitment, humanity could overcome obstacles and create a world where every individual could flourish.

New-Way Learning System

Learning perpetuates societal progress.

The learning system should serve as a societal beacon. Learning is a lifelong endeavor that begins with formal schooling and extends to continuous lifelong skill acquisition. To ensure sustainability, learning must be practical, contextually relevant, and guided by spirituality for *Life's Larger Context.*

The below quick statistics based on incomes, as obtained from UNESCO, reveal a complex global learning landscape with significant but substantial challenges remaining, particularly in achieving fair access:

Learning Measure	High-Income	Low-Income
Literacy Rate	> 98%	About 70%
Advanced Tech in Schools	> 90%	< 40%
Completion Rate	> 70%	< 40%
Spending per Student	About $11k	> $400

Vish believed in the spiritual "*reflect and reset*" philosophy. From time to time, one should reflect on one's actions and reset positions as necessary based on humane considerations and developing contexts.

Sparq spearheaded the New-Way Learning movement, which emphasized holistic learning and earnest application of education and skills. "The New-Way Learning system will answer the questions of what, why, when, and how of the learning processes for our consequence-driven society," Sparq stated.

The system empowered individuals with knowledge and skills, enabling them to thrive in various personal, social, academic, and professional contexts. All education and skill without practice or application would neither utilize human potential nor benefit society.

Sparq reminded everyone of Vish's emphasis: "Everyone should work according to their ability. Learning is to gain knowledge and skill, to act with conscience, and to return justice and opportunity back to society." The focal point was advancing both knowledge and skills while instilling values such as empathy, inclusiveness, tolerance, and sympathetic joy.

The New-Way Learning policy created frameworks that played fundamental roles in shaping individuals and societies, driving balanced and sustainable progress. Through education, students gained abilities in reflection, collaboration, innovation, and responsibility. The curriculum focuses on human well-being with progressive but sustainable advancement.

"The universal achievement of basic skills—proficiency in reading, writing, speaking, and ability to use current tools—has tremendous potential for citizen participation in a country's progress to ensure sustainable growth," Sparq explained.

Education - Fundamental Human Right

New-Way Governance included Education in its basic sustenance CHEFS (Clothing, Healthcare, *Education*, Food, Shelter) policy.

Free universal children's education provided up to adulthood or grade schooling. Then follows Four years of mandatory undergraduate college education at subsidized fees with repayment required four years after course completion.

College education focused on areas covering national needs under the umbrella of primal constructs. The system offered flexibility through hybrid learning environments, with both in-person and remote options available (though grade schooling remained in-person only).

Learning after graduate school was at a cost that can be paid either by learners, guardians or donors using their personal LifeScores. Early college education costs were highly discounted to ensure more people get minimum higher education affordably. The Colleges for Advanced Higher Education implemented a progressive fee structure:

- Talented students received higher subsidies.
- Higher LifeScore meant access to higher education.
- Parents or sponsors could spend their LifeScores.
- Students earned LifeScores through volunteer work.

Anyone of any age could access learning from master learning catalogs managed by governments in collaboration with local communities.

Adit's pioneering work created the transformative Master Catalog system—a platform empowering communities and governments. These groundbreaking real-time catalogs were updated continuously based on citizen feedback, addressing local and national needs. By harnessing collective wisdom, the Master Catalogs became the pinnacle of collaborative problem-solving tools.

In New-Way Ideology, a country's progress was measured by how much advanced learning its citizens could access, pursue, accomplish, sustain, and practice. Administration at various levels determined needs and priorities for funding learning infrastructures, considering what was basic, advanced, and needed for present and future.

Learning Providers

Dr. Sparq organized the Learning System into two complementary components – Providers and Services:

Education Providers (Physical Infrastructure)

Delivered curriculum and created conducive learning environments.

Quantum Information Processing (QIP) operates smart facilities.

Administered personalized learning with instant feedback mechanisms.

Managed libraries as knowledge repository platforms linking to humanity's digitized knowledge—the 'Akashic Records.'

Education Services (Human and AI Elements)

Created content and imparted education and skills.

Tailored pedagogies to individual student needs.

Provided tutoring, mentoring, career counseling, and assessment services.

Delivered teaching, guidance, and support across all learning levels.

Teaching rose as a prestigious profession in the New-Way system. "The New-Way Learning System aims to establish teaching as a prestigious, meaningful, and impactful career path," Sparq highlighted. "Doing so will continue to draw brilliant minds to nurture the next generation, fuel academic pursuits, and empower communities while boosting their own LifeScores."

Teachers, instructors, coaches, authors, counselors, and mentors all received additive LifeScores based on Skills and accomplishments, Service quality and dedication, Impact on mentees and Contribution to nation-building.

New-Way Governance acknowledged the necessity of maintaining a great pool of teachers and educators at all education and learning levels. The government created exclusive higher education institutions for teachers, imparting advanced skills and training methods. Sparq and Lea conducted extensive research spanning:

Ancient Learning methods: Mesopotamian, Vedic, Buddhist, Chinese, Greek, and Arabic

Medieval educational philosophies and methods
Modern models from Finland, Denmark, and South Korea
Synthesis of historical wisdom with contemporary needs

Sparq and Core Team aimed to develop progressive learning frameworks that synthesized timeless wisdom while meeting current and future needs.

Ms. Sparq, with invaluable Core Team assistance, meticulously crafted the New-Way Education policy to be self-sufficient, all-inclusive, and ever-evolving. The resulting research paper, "The Document on New-Way Learning," served as the definitive guideline for New-Way governments. Key implementation features included:

State-funded learning support systems.
Train-the-trainer programs for teaching professionals.
Performance metrics based on real-world and societal impact.
Integration with the global vision of humanity's well-being.
Opportunities for students to earn LifeScores while learning through volunteer work and internships.

Sparq explained a critical principle: "Learning outdated or ineffectual knowledge is resources not well spent and not useful to society." New-Way governments collaborated globally to determine relevant knowledge areas.

Through these integrated systems of education, healthcare, and philanthropy, the New-Way movement created a comprehensive framework for human flourishing. By aligning individual aspirations with collective needs, ensuring universal access to essential services, and fostering a culture of giving back, New-Way societies unleashed humanity's collective potential for a sustainable and equitable future.

***

Empathy and Fairness

Every living person has the right to clothing, health, education, food, and shelter.

Grace Core CHEFS Team member was from Namibia. This was the land that witnessed profound human suffering. As a descendant of Herero survivors of the early 20th-century genocide, her heritage bore the scars of dispossession, deportation, forced labor, racial segregation, and discrimination inflicted by colonists. This tragedy was regarded as the first genocide of the 20th century. Recently, justice was partially served when reparations were awarded to the descendants of the victims. Large sums were awarded to the surviving people, marking a significant step toward acknowledging past atrocities.

Vish envisioned a world where citizens should not have to worry about meeting their basic life essentials. In such a world, where these essentials were assured, people could devote their time to more meaningful pursuits.

"He wished humanity to have guaranteed subsistence because everyone is born with those rights," Ms. Grace explained. Elaborating on Vish's ideology, Grace concluded, "Yet the New-Way thinking also compels citizens to work hard for sustained well-being and progress."

Vish had recognized a critical challenge: guaranteed subsistence could potentially lead to catastrophic idleness. To address this, he designed innovative mechanisms that incentivized active contribution while preventing widespread complacency. Dr. Grace emphasized how LifeScore, combined with concepts like No-Inheritance, served as powerful motivators inspiring individuals to engage in meaningful work.

This philosophy resonated deeply in 22nd century Namibia. Many beneficiaries from the Herero and Nama communities generously donated their reparation funds to humanitarian causes and New-Way Ideology propagation. Grace herself became a major donor, dedicating her efforts to advancing the movement throughout Namibia and other African nations.

From her home in Walvis Bay—a town perched on the edge of the Namib Desert at the mouth of the Kuiseb River—Grace balanced her research with a passion for birdwatching. The bay's abundant wildlife, including flamingos, pelicans, and Damara Terns, perfectly suited her interests. She kept various binoculars at hand, ready to observe these seasonal visitors whenever she stepped away from the laboratory.

On this day, Grace flew from Walvis Bay Airport to Hosea Kutako International Airport in Windhoek, Namibia's capital. Her ultimate destination was Bloemfontein, where she would meet Dr. YoloMunk to study young John's case. However, she had arranged a strategic stopover in Windhoek to join a gathering of Core

Team members: Mr. Antony Lubo, Ms. Beti Amira, Ms. Veronica Clark, Mr. Paul Tempr, and Ms. Lea.

Mr. Antony Lubo was from the capital city, Gaborone of Botswana, a liberal country.

Ms. Beti Amira was from Rwanda. She was a parliamentarian and also an expert in traditional highly choreographed Intore dance.

Ms. Veronica Clark was from Niger, the largest and poorest country in West Africa. In her childhood, she worked in the uranium ore mines.

Mr. Paul Tempr was an Amazigh from Morocco, representing the indigenous people of North Africa from the Maghreb region.

Coffee, Tea, and Philosophy

The meeting took place at the home of Paul's close friend in Olympia, an affluent neighborhood in East Windhoek. Nine people gathered, including Paul the host, Antony, Veronica, Beti, Paul's friend Ms. Rooky, and Grace. Lea and Lin would join them within the hour, having just landed at Hosea Kutako International Airport.

The attendees shared a common bond with Grace—histories of deprivation, oppression, and humble beginnings that made her accomplishments even more meaningful to them.

Grace opened the discussion by tracing humanity's progression. "Humans evolved from securing food for survival, to clothing for dignity, to shelter for safety, to healthcare for wellness, and finally to education for sustained well-being," she explained. "Now that we've achieved guaranteed subsistence, humanity's urgent need in the 22nd century is climate protection on earth and in near space for the safety and preservation of our species."

She noted that historically, only small segments of the global population had benefited from progress. New-Way Ideology aimed to change this fundamental inequality.

Grace clarified the critical distinction between subsistence and sustenance. Subsistence levels provided minimum CHEFS allocations necessary for basic survival. Sustenance mechanisms went beyond mere survival—they included fair budgetary allocations and LifeScore implementation that guaranteed CHEFS provisioning while enabling citizens to thrive spiritually and emotionally.

Under New-Way Ideology, these basic needs became a social guarantee. Governments assumed full responsibility for their citizens' welfare, allocating 100% funding for subsistence needs. The minimum education standard was set at twelve grade years.

As one of Africa's freest and most democratic countries, Namibia had made a straightforward choice to embrace New-Way Ideology—considered the most humane and progressive ideology in human history.

Mr. Antony Lubo, Ms. Beti Amira, Ms. Veronica Clark, and Mr. Paul Tempr had gained continent-wide recognition as prominent activists. Working closely with Dr. Grace Rukaro, they spearheaded systemic changes throughout Namibia.

Paul served the group, roasting and grinding coffee beans before them. The fresh, distinct aroma filled the room. Ms. Rooky had brought Grace's recommendations—coffee beans from North Africa and tea from the South.

During her sessions with Grace's local team, Lea enjoyed the tea immensely, drinking from a cup that locals found amusingly oversized. She was reading her book "The Theory of Social Everything" which had resonated across many nations.

"Aristotle may have said man is a social animal," Lea observed, "but over time, man has evolved into an unsocial animal." She explained that Vish's concept of evolved human well-being fundamentally addressed collective welfare through an emotionally agnostic approach.

In New-Way countries, the institutionalized LifeScore mechanism automatically recognized all actions and efforts. To protect system integrity, Lea and Lin developed a failsafe feedback mechanism preventing corruption and deception.

"The new paradigm—*disconnected but united*—ensures people don't build fragile egos that crumble like houses of cards in our emotionally charged world," Lea explained. Under this system, people no longer sought validation outside the LifeScore framework.

The group—Grace, Lea, Paul, Veronica, Beti, and Antony—continued discussing New-Way Ideology implementation in Namibia. They examined wellness and social changes in detail, noting that Namibia's transformation had followed Uruguay's successful transition.

Grace concluded by declaring that New-Way Ideology, with its revolutionary approaches to Economy, Politics, and Society, had proven instrumental in these countries' success. The gathering represented not just a meeting of minds, but a celebration of progress from shared struggles to collective triumph.

Safety and Security Framework

After the meeting concluded in Olympia, an affluent district of Windhoek, Grace and Lea departed from Ms. Rooky's residence around 12:30 AM. They took a taxi to Lea's hotel near Eros Airport.

Their driver, Lima, proved remarkably friendly. She enthusiastically described her taxi's emission-free technology, explaining that her friend—an environmental engineer—had developed engines superior to electric or hydrogen alternatives in terms of end-to-end ecosystem pollution. While Grace and Lea couldn't verify this technology, they appreciated Lima's evident pride in contributing to a carbon-free environment.

The next morning, Grace and Lea met in the lobby before proceeding to the hotel's open-air breakfast terrace. Adonis, the front desk attendant, seated them at a table with a splendid mountain view. She placed a basket of fresh whole wheat bread on their table, saying, "Have a nice breakfast! A waiter will be with you shortly."

The terrace offered a cozy atmosphere with scenic views of the surrounding mountains—neither too distant nor imposingly high, they encircled the city with natural beauty. The women ordered local breakfast items from the snack basket, fruit basket, and freshly roasted gourmet coffee selections.

"Is there a phase in evolution that's without safety and security?" Grace pondered aloud. "People prosper because they have safety and security."

She distinguished between the two concepts: safety protects individuals from unintentional harm, while security shields them from intentional threats. Both prove crucial for human well-being, providing foundations for individuals and societies to thrive through—Physical safety, Emotional well-being, social participation, Economic prosperity and Human rights protection.

Grace referenced New-Way Hierarchy of Needs, noting that safety was ranked as the second most fundamental human need after physiological necessities. Without safety, individuals cannot progress toward self-actualization. She also mentioned how Vish got Safety and Security as birth right entitlement as part of CHEFS program.

The Core Team developed comprehensive frameworks for Safety and Security, recognizing that threats emerge from both human and natural sources. Man-made threats included: Environmental destruction, Interpersonal violence and Indifference to collective well-being

"These threats can be mitigated when people understand the consequences and act conscientiously," Grace explained.

She emphasized the importance of individual participation, drawing parallels to military principles: 'Just as soldiers uphold the ethic of all-for-one and one-for-all, we too must keep our communities united, with members supporting one another.

"Economic backwardness makes everything more difficult," Grace observed, noting how people tend to prioritize personal survival. Limited progress bred skepticism toward government intentions and policies.

The New-Way Core Team created comprehensive guidelines addressing—Natural disasters, Extinction-level events and Outer space colony protocols.

These guidelines applied universally, whether on Earth or in space colonies. Following Vish's directive to "*Preserve humaneness at all costs*," they prioritized safety and security more than anything else. As Vish famously wrote: "*You act humanely when you feel safe and secure*!"

The Core Team recognized that people feel secure when surrounded by those willing to help others first. Once basic needs are met, people naturally think beyond survival toward desires and aspirations.

"Wishing for an idealistic society isn't enough to build one," Grace acknowledged. Therefore, the Core Team developed practical policies and frameworks for New-Way governments, setting clear expectations using guiding principles to foster hardworking, interdependent cultures.

"Social threats include greed, mistrust, jealousy, and selfishness—resulting in harassment and physical aggression among other ills," Grace noted. "We achieve safety and security by addressing and removing these negative traits."

Grace and Lea created guiding principles transforming simple acts of social participation into powerful tools against major social threats. These principles and actions possessed both universal appeal and practical applicability, forming the foundation for safer, more secure New-Way societies.

Dignity and Respect

Grace understood a fundamental truth: wealth alone could not buy dignity and respect. These qualities were earned through good deeds and in New-Way living directly measured by LifeScore. In the 22nd century, those with higher LifeScore values commanded dignity and respect in all their interactions, whether direct or indirect. Such was the ubiquitous role of LifeScore in New-Way societies.

Lea and Grace collaborated extensively on bringing dignity and respect to everyone's lives, despite their vastly different personal backgrounds. Lea was born into a wealthy, orthodox Catholic family and never struggled for worldly necessities—a stark contrast to Grace's brush with extreme hardship. Yet Lea's innate compassion drew her to New-Way Ideology during her college years. Like other Core Team members, she believed New-Way philosophy offered precise solutions for humanity's leap into the 22nd century and beyond.

In her book "Theory of Social Everything," Lea acknowledged how technology had transformed human interaction. For the first time in history, humans could lead entirely remote social lives without physical or even eye contact. This transformation was enabled by:

- Advanced holography.
- Digital transactions.
- Procreation without physical intimacy.
- Messaging-to-brain technology.
- Auto-discovery of emotions.

In New-Way countries, physical violence has become uncommon; killings were extremely rare. The family system had evolved into *cohabitation-on-consent*. People were encouraged to think independently while prioritizing collective good.

Following the principle "Give Respect and Take Respect," the New-Way system treated everyone with inherent dignity. As Grace defined it:

Dignity: The ability to be yourself
Respect: What others recognize in you
LifeScore: The unique measure embodying both hard work and helpfulness

Working with Maria and Lea, Grace transformed abstract notions of dignity and respect into objective LifeScore measurements. Vish's vision ensured LifeScore made no distinctions based on race or physical attributes or such divisions—only actions and consequences mattered.

Breaking Historical Discrimination

Until the 22nd century, all countries perpetuated some form of discrimination based on:

Race and caste, Class and nationality, Sexual orientation, Skin color, Age and religion.

Grace understood this intimately as a descendant of the Herero people who faced genocide. Africa had particularly suffered from centuries of discrimination against girls and women.

Grace established multiple organizations to combat discrimination:

Equal Girl Africa Inc. (EGAI)

- Led by Grace and Kirl
- Focused on girls' education.
- Provided supplies, clothing, food, tutoring, and healthcare.
- Secured parental and societal support.
- Operated through local school districts.

Quality Health Africa Inc. (QHAI)
Led by Grace and Sparq
Focused on population health.
Served Middle Eastern and African countries.

Grace led healthcare initiatives while Sparq enabled educational access. They created educational and financial trusts managing projects for minorities and vulnerable populations. They donated substantial amounts to corpus funds while Kirl offered spiritual guidance to members.

These organizations achieved tangible results at grassroots levels. Their efforts brought equality to girls and women across Namibia and other African countries. Success of these initiatives was measured by:

- Women and girls taking part from all levels of society.
- Established safety and security for females.
- Higher education achievement rates.
- Improved health outcomes.
- Realizing dignity and respect in daily life.

Through New-Way Governance implementation, earning dignity and respect became reality for common people within the same generation, transforming abstract ideals into lived experience across Africa.

LifeScore Philosophy

"Hard work is the basis for progress. Without hard work, spectacular things would not happen," Grace commented. "Mundane actions are routine things we do every day without much effort or stress. These lead to normal, unremarkable routines and outcomes." She used the example of picking up children from school as a typical mundane action.

In New-Way communities, earning better things requires hard work. It was the only way to increase one's LifeScore, which ultimately qualified a person for better material benefits. Those who realized that only hard work paid off earned significant personal achievements and greater respect, as reflected in their LifeScores.

Grace believed that *what was due to a person was directly proportional to their participation in and contribution to society.* This principle was reflected proportionately in LifeScore assignments. LifeScore, which for the first time in human history codified and valued the existence of human life, was defined as the "Sum of Actions for Self and for Selfless." The system valued actions with weights and qualifiers (+add/-subtract/×multiply) that corresponded to the community in which people lived.

"There are selfless and spiritual actions that benefit others," Grace explained. "These actions that benefit others and that connect and bind people together in real and metaphysical ways are valued higher than actions for self. Selfish actions are abhorred in the New-Way way of living. Lazy people get dismal LifeScores."

Vish had shown the path through an ideology that had already achieved success in the early 22nd century across the globe. His seminal work on New-Way Ideology was based on Humanology and Consequentialism, rooted in human well-being. This ideology had foundations in liberalism, progressivism, collectivism, and general well-being.

"According to Vish, in a cause-and-effect paradigm, human existence is the cause, and human actions and consequent results are the effects," Grace stated. This ideology contradicted philosophies such as Karma, Destiny, and the traditional Meaning of Life. Grace, along with the Core Team and her team from Africa, drew out an elaborate treatise detailing examples of hard work and related accomplishments. She pointed to man-made wonders, technological achievements, social revolutions, and political adjustments from human history to motivate people to continue working hard.

"No hard work goes to waste, it always shows results," Grace emphasized, quoting Vish: "*Hard work is the cause and Change is the effect.*"

The Carrot and Stick of LifeScore

Grace understood the fragile nature of human beings who could easily slip into the abyss of laziness in the new age of guaranteed subsistence. She firmly believed LifeScore was a simple yet powerful guiding formula for people to follow the right path. Grace and her team had further codified a straightforward checklist for citizens to follow, ensuring they worked hard in their daily lives according to their abilities and skills.

Using the carrot and stick analogy, LifeScore served as the singular representation for both. The higher one's LifeScore, the bigger the carrot, a better life sweetened with increased entitlements. Conversely, the lower one's LifeScore, the longer the stick, a bare minimum existence, a bitter life with fewer things that left one wanting more.

This deprivation, when managed positively, compelled people to choose to work harder.

Grace passionately believed that by dangling this carrot of rewards for hard work while administering the stick of scarcity for laziness, the LifeScore system motivated people. It kept them striving to improve their scores through diligent efforts according to their potential.

Grace and her team in Namibia participated in planning sessions to create innovative public works programs:

- *Food-for-work*: Paid workers in food supplies
- *Cash-for-work*: Paid workers in monetary compensation.
- *Score-for-Spirituality*: Rewarded LifeScore measures for spiritual work such as teaching, research, leadership, entrepreneurship, and meditation.

These programs achieved remarkable success with multiple benefits. They made people work hard and showed them ways to earn higher LifeScores and attain greater benefits. The programs addressed issues like directionless and goalless lives. The programs created and funded public works in the economy, resulting in increased economic transactions. These initiatives had proven to raise incomes for individuals, families, and communities throughout New-Way countries, helping meet various material needs of the population.

The success was truly multi-faceted. People found purpose and direction through the incentive of earning a higher LifeScore. Their hard work benefited not only themselves but also drove economic and social activity. As incomes rose, people could afford more of their essential needs. Entire communities prospered from the productive efforts of motivated citizens striving for better LifeScore ratings. The programs uplifted societies comprehensively giving people goals, fostering self-reliance, generating economic growth, and elevating living standards. This served as a true testament to the core New-Way principles.

At the policy framework level, these programs possessed distinct advantages. They effectively targeted low-income and low-LifeScore populations and encouraged local economic growth by supporting local food producers and economies. The programs strengthened long-term food security by improving local infrastructure, manufacturing activities, and agricultural potential.

Grace ensured these programs collaborated with various government bodies and local community projects. Agriculture, horticulture, dairy, manufacturing, and other economic sectors all benefited from these initiatives. Working with Adit's algorithms, Grace ensured that participation and hard work were accurately captured in the LifeScore metric, guaranteeing that the population received due entitlements and rewards.

Vish had drawn up the LifeScore formula to make people work for themselves while simultaneously motivating them to work for others as well. The inherent nature of entitlements and rewards made people get up and work. The harder one worked, the sweeter the results one enjoyed. New-Way Governments created comprehensive plans to reward people for their hard work based on their LifeScores.

The Ingenious Scoring System

The LifeScore calculation system was particularly clever. Work was categorized as either for self or for selfless reasons. Rewards were mapped out along with weightage assigned by local committees based on their community needs.

The calculation gave higher weightage to selfless acts that benefited others and the community. Work that helped only oneself received lower weightage. Local committees determined the critical needs of their community and assigned higher weightages to work that addressed those key needs. This ensured people's efforts were directed toward areas of greatest importance for their specific community.

The rewards mapped to LifeScore were quite enticing. Higher scores unlocked access to premium facilities, luxuries, and community recognition. Lower scores meant only basic amenities. This system motivated people to work hard, especially on selfless acts that their community valued highly. The LifeScore system deftly coupled individual aspirations with collective needs through an ingenious incentive structure that benefited both the individual and society.

LifeScore entitled a person to certain worldly things such as a Bike, a Car, and a House with varying degrees of luxury attached. Grace gave some examples:

The following Actions provided a good weightage and better score:

- Driving to get own groceries
- Construction of own house
- Teaching own children

- Farming for own consumption

Below Actions offered a high weightage and higher score:

- Teaching in Institutions
- Providing healthcare at hospitals
- Working on cooperative farming
- Researching in labs
- Earning medals in sports
- Earning recognition for their communities
- Giving spiritual discourses
- Enduring hardship for the benefit of others

"The value system of rewards and penalties evolved with times and individual societies since people and cultures valued things differently over time," Grace said. Grace opined, "LifeScore and CHEFS implementation seemed like a mechanism that was taking the place of systems like Capitalism, Communism, or Socialism all at once." She mentioned what Vish prophesied, "It's time to sound the death knell to Capitalism, Communism, or Socialism." Vish said, "LifeScore is a *Just* System for fairness and equality!"

Lea and Grace were knowledgeable bloggers who extensively wrote and discussed "Just Entitlements and Fair Rewards" in the context of New-Way modern life in the 22nd century.

In the New-Way system, entitlements were benefits and rights that individuals received based on their deeds. Rewards were granted as recognition for individual achievements, represented by one component of the LifeScore formula that factored in hard work and efforts toward self-improvement. The systematization of both entitlements and rewards served as powerful motivators for people to engage in activities, helping both themselves and society at large.

Grace reminded everyone of Vish's fundamental definition: "Human Life is defined as the Sum of Actions for Self and Selfless." She explained that those incapable of contributing to their own survival received a Child score, signifying their need for higher attention and care. Additionally, Vish had designed the system so that each society could customize and tailor the LifeScore formula to fit its members' specific needs.

Grace strongly advocated Vish's LifeScore system, believing it offered a fair and just means of recognizing and rewarding individuals based solely on their actions and consequences. She collaborated with the Core Team to create a comprehensive treatise documenting various achievements mapping their corresponding entitlements and rewards. These achievements encompassed claims to both tangible and intangible possessions, as well as claims to respect and dignity.

The LifeScore Platform

Through the LifeScore platform, individuals could experience genuine inclusion in coveted realms of society. A higher score provided flexibility to choose preferred types of work and offered access to prestigious awards and medals of honor. Each person's score was meticulously recorded, stored, and updated in real-time, enabling efficient administration of entitlements and rewards. Adit proved instrumental in developing the technological framework for this system, which earned praise for its ubiquity, integrity, and user-friendliness.

Grace acknowledged the necessity of social safety net programs to aid the population. The LifeScore platform addressed multiple needs—providing impetus, encouragement, inducement, inspiration, and justification for individuals to labor for the betterment of self and others. Vish had recognized the challenge of inspiring diligent work for others' benefit when essential sustenance requirements were already guaranteed. His solution was to define the New-Way living work ethic for the material benefits.

Adit's technological architecture and implementation framework facilitated data gathering from various sources through sensors. The data then updated and vetted by the respective communities. This is implemented as a real-time feedback activity. His algorithms consolidated and evaluated information to generate the metrics and measurements necessary for LifeScore programs. Meanwhile, Grace, Lea, and other Core Team members formulated policy guidelines for categorizing and assigning value to work, which were seamlessly integrated into the LifeScore system.

The Core Team understood that community involvement was crucial to the system's success. Citizens and council members would access LifeScore metric as per their privilege to provide feedback and participation. Community leaders played significant roles in providing input on the classification and categorization of parametric items, ensuring the community had the final say on work participation components.

Just Reward and Resource Allocation

Vish's vision for an equitable society centered on the concept of 'just rewards and fair entitlements.' By requiring hard work and achievements for social benefits, individuals were acknowledged and compensated for their contributions. Resources and opportunities were allocated based on merit rather than social status or privilege.

The Core Team developed policy guidelines for the subsistence budget, based on community-specific estimates. As an example:

Shelter: 25%
Healthcare: 15%
Food: 15%
Transportation: 15%
Learning: 10%
Clothing: 8%
Miscellaneous expenses: 7%
Entertainment: 5%

These allocations were subject to slight variations depending on local community needs and circumstances.

Grace clarified an important distinction: the LifeScore mechanism applied only to individuals who had attained adulthood (those who were able-bodied and over 18 years of age). To obtain rewards and awards based on the LifeScore formula, adult citizens had to work for them. She emphasized the crucial role of CHEFS in fulfilling children's basic needs, ensuring that minors receive full support regardless of their ability to contribute to the LifeScore system.

This approach created a comprehensive framework where adults were motivated to contribute while children remained fully protected and supported—embodying the New-Way principle of balancing individual responsibility with collective care.

***

Peaceful Life

Peace is living in safety and freedom.

In the iconic city of Hamburg, a remarkable event occurred that would reverberate through the realms of art, philosophy, and human consciousness itself. It was a performance by two towering figures whose impact on the world cannot be overstated—Kirl, the esteemed Russian mathematician and gentle philosopher, and Rawpwr, the globally renowned musician whose lyrics and melodies have captivated hearts across the globe. This show became a symphony of creativity, wisdom, and artistic expression, resonating far beyond the hallowed walls of the Elbphilharmonie concert hall where it took place.

Kirl, revered worldwide for his profound insights into the nature of existence, had become particularly influential in all of Europe and Asia. Known for his unwavering commitment to seven fundamental social values—Dignity, Fairness, Compassion, Integrity, Freedom, Solidarity, and Respect—Kirl illuminated the path toward harmonious coexistence and personal transformation.

On this evening, the Elbphilharmonie's Grand Hall transformed into a captivating canvas of color, haze, and anticipation as Rawpwr took the stage before an audience of over 2,100 enraptured souls. His entrance was a spectacle unto itself, a burst of energy that ignited the crowd's fervor. As he strode onto the stage in his signature attire, a momentary hush fell over the audience.

And then, the music began.

Rawpwr's artistry flowed like a river of emotion, each note a droplet in a cascading torrent of sound that swept the audience into its embrace. He moved seamlessly between guitar, flute, and piano, each instrument revealing a different facet of his musical creative genius. His sound blended diverse cultures and traditions into one unified expression. His style transcended genres and boundaries, resonating with listeners of all backgrounds, for in his music lay a universal truth, a language that spoke directly to the soul.

For three hours, the audience remained spellbound, their spirits soaring on the wings of Rawpwr's artistry. Then came an unexpected moment, Kirl, though not known as a performer, joined in with hip-hop lyrics and singing. The crowd erupted in ecstatic appreciation, seeing Kirl's first-ever participation in a musical performance. They valued him not for artistic prowess but for his many humanitarian contributions and plain honesty.

The magnetic pull of Rawpwr's artistry stemmed from his lyrical mastery—words that intertwined profound depth with subtle nuance and visceral emotion, lending gravity to every theme he touched. These lyrics weren't mere accompaniments but the very soul of his creative vision, binding him to followers across a vast spectrum of humanity—rich and poor, young and old, from every corner of the earth. Within his verses, listeners discovered reflections of their personal journeys, their victories and defeats, their unspoken dreams and deepest yearnings.

As the performance ended, Rawpwr and Kirl did Namaste, offering a benediction of peace. The shared experience had transcended entertainment, becoming a moment of solidarity and respect.

As the crowd dispersed, still glowing from the experience, Kirl sought out Rawpwr. Their bond was built on mutual respect—Kirl admired Rawpwr's musical reach to millions, while Rawpwr valued Kirl's profound understanding of society's deepest challenges.

In a symbolic exchange, Kirl presented Rawpwr with *the Book*, a book that had profoundly influenced both men's worldviews. Seeking solace in nature, the two friends ventured to a local park, walking briskly for two miles along the serene Elbe River waterfront. Donning caps to partially obscure their identities, they relished the opportunity to connect without public recognition, their conversation flowing as freely as the river beside them.

Here, amidst tranquility, they engaged in profound discourse on New-Way Ideology—a philosophy transcending borders and cultures. They acknowledged how Vish's teachings emphasized respect and dignity for all beings, echoing the Prime Directive principle from "Star Trek" that all sentient life deserves compassion and understanding.

Yet Vish's vision extended beyond human interaction to encompass reverence for the natural world—water, land, air, and space. He advocated preserving these elements in their pristine state, maintaining the delicate balance between humanity and nature for future generations.

Kirl championed the principle of 'reflect and reset'—dedicating time to contemplation, meditation, and intellectual discourse to gain deeper insights, then transforming these revelations into tangible works: harmonious structures, soul-stirring art, or groundbreaking research.

For Kirl, this creative manifestation was the ultimate expression of Vish's philosophy—a testament to the symbiotic relationship between inner reflection and outward manifestation of contemplation and action.

As night drew to a close and the friends parted, their bond had strengthened through shared reverence for Vish's teachings and commitment to using their talents to inspire humanity. The following evening at 5 PM, Kirl would deliver his much-anticipated lecture at Hall 424 Jürgen Carstensen e. K., continuing the symphony of wisdom and artistic expression begun that night.

Despite the late hour, the companions rose early, eager to immerse themselves in Hamburg's vibrant heart. They got together at a charming restaurant for leisurely brunch, where conversation flowed as freely as the aroma of freshly brewed coffee. Fed in body and spirit, they grabbed to-go coffees and strolled toward Hall 424 Jürgen Carstensen e. K., where Kirl was scheduled to lecture. The twenty-minute walk afforded them the perfect opportunity to bask in the city's ambiance.

Upon arriving at the non-descript hall, they settled into the speakers' lounge. Here Rawpwr conceived an innovative experience—seamlessly blending music and philosophy into harmonious convergence of artistic expression and intellectual discourse.

As attendees arrived, they encountered an intriguing sight. Virtual figures appeared through holoportation technology, mingling effortlessly with flesh-and-blood participants. This ambitious undertaking created an atmosphere of inclusivity transcending physical boundaries.

With the stage set, Kirl took the podium. His gentle demeanor and profound insights captivated all present. "Spirituality plays a crucial role in every individual's journey," Kirl emphasized. He highlighted the significance of one's place within the global society. Quoting Vish, he recounted, "*You are what others think you are.*" For it is the collective strength of society's members, exerted upon one another, that shapes community fabric. Kirl urged channeling this powerful social influence for humanity's greater good, transcending any single society's boundaries.

During the lively question-and-answer session, hands rose not only from the gathered crowd but from far-flung corners of the globe. Through holoportation, participants even from distant space colonies joined the discourse, bridging vast distances in testament to technology's potential to unite minds and hearts.

Throughout his life, Kirl had dedicated himself to teaching and investing energy into public projects uplifting the human spirit—planetariums, observatories, libraries, and science cities. His efforts left an indelible mark on numerous European countries and elsewhere, a legacy born from unwavering belief in Vish's ideology: "Life is ephemeral but powerful. Use it for the benefit of all in the larger context of humanity's benefit."

As *Viswas*, Vish's virtual confidant, noted: 'Kirl knows that various current social systems have become self-centric and detrimental to society at large.' Kirl echoed this sentiment, lamenting how economic, political, and social systems had become so entangled in self-interest that they fostered cultures of greed and short-sightedness.

Viswas then shared Vish's cosmic theory: 'Stellar objects ever move away from each other until their matter dissipates, only to re-emerge elsewhere in the universe. It's a never-ending alternating cycle of construction and destruction.

Inspired by this cosmic vision, Kirl challenged his audience to reach for humanity's highest potential. The choice lies with everyone—to build up or tear down our collective potential.

As the day closed and attendees dispersed, both physical and virtual, intellectual and spiritual nourishment lingered. Kirl's words, intertwined with Rawpwr's jazz accompaniment, had spread an enlightenment inviting all to embrace patience, kindness, diversity, and inclusiveness.

For Kirl and Rawpwr, this meeting was not merely a talent convergence but harmonious prelude to greater journeys of self-discovery and societal transformation. Their collaboration touched many lives, planting wisdom seeds that would continue blooming long after departure.

New-Way Sanctuary Centers (NSC)

Diversity and inclusiveness are necessary conditions for life.

Have you ever encountered someone whose mere presence radiates serenity and compassion? A soul whose gentle demeanor and profound wisdom instantly puts you at ease. If so, you may have crossed paths with Kirl, whose unwavering commitment to kindness and peace has left an indelible mark on countless lives.

Guided by New-Way Ideology, Kirl dedicated his life to promoting peace, tolerance, and the cultivation of a harmonious society. At the heart of his philosophy lay a simple yet powerful truth attributed to Plato: 'Be kind, for everyone you meet is fighting a harder battle.'

These words resonated deeply within Kirl, for he understood that beneath our daily interactions lay unseen struggles. This realization fueled his tireless efforts creating a global network of sanctuaries—"New-Way Sanctuary Centers" where individuals find respite, reconnect with nature, and re-engage in transformative practices of meditation, contemplation, and virtuous deeds.

Imagine stepping into one of these serenity oases. One such Sanctuary Center was along the border of Uruguay and Brazil. Here, you're invited to immerse yourself in nature's restorative embrace, wandering paths through lush landscapes mimicking local biomes. Panic grass, pennywort, and golden daisies carpet the ground, while Cockspur coral trees, Humboldt's willows, Sarandí Colorados, and Talas offer shade canopies. These carefully curated ecosystems transport you to realms of inner peace.

Exploring further, you might discover tranquil waters of a mini-aquatic biome between Uruguay and Brazil. Fishing is prohibited, allowing diverse marine life to thrive undisturbed. Schools of Pejerreyes, Los pintados, Wolf fish, and various catfish species navigate crystalline depths—living testaments to preservation's importance.

But these Sanctuary centers offer more than escape—they're sanctuaries of learning, growth, and transformation. Vast meditation domes accommodate up to 2,000 individuals for contemplation. Intimate debating rooms each for 30 people foster discourse and idea exchange, allowing diverse perspectives to intermingle and inspire.

At this centers' heart were dedicated staff—Nicolas, Sofia, Francisco, Lucia, Bruno, Camila, Lucas, and Florencia—embodying Vish's teachings. Their commitment to tolerance, kindness, and compassion was rewarded with handsome LifeScores, the tangible measures of positive societal impact.

Simply spending time in these centers contributes to LifeScores, while active helpers and facilitators earn higher weightings for their efforts that create lasting harmony that leaves a profound impact on society. Local governments sponsor NSC infrastructure while Kirl, Lea, and Sparq representing New-Way collaborate on policy frameworks. New-Way governments embrace these principles, recognizing centers' benefits—improved health, inner peace, and LifeScore boosts.

Kirl understands Vish's ideology is neither utopian nor unrealistic—it's a practical philosophy balancing freedom and choice with necessary guardrails. These safeguards manifest through LifeScore metrics and the New-Way Justice System, ensuring unfettered volition doesn't lead to societal harm.

As Viswas explains: "LifeScore makes people strive toward tolerance, kindness, and compassion. Its mechanisms deter paths benefiting only self or harming others."

In this harmonious symphony of kindness, Sanctuary centers serve as orchestras, staff as musicians, and visitors as the appreciative but participating audience. Everyone passing through the center joins this grand performance, contributing their unique voice to the evolving melodies of growth and transformation.

The Art of Giving and Receiving

One's best self is when one is a graceful recipient and a kinder donor.

These words from Vish reverberate through *Viswas*, his trusted and omniscient virtual confidant. Within this statement lies harmonious society's essence—where giving and receiving transcend mere transaction.

The Core Team understands philanthropy's profound significance as genuine goodwill manifestation. Kirl particularly embodies this spirit, his empathy reservoir knowing no bounds, continually seeking ways to uplift others. He recognizes that equity, justice, and freedom aren't abstract concepts but essential foundations for a compassionate society.

With unwavering commitment, Kirl collaborated with Lea and Maria developing comprehensive frameworks for institutionalizing philanthropy within New-Way Ideology. From this emerged the New-Way Sanctuary Centers (NSC), an apex institution designed not merely facilitating generosity but embodying one's highest, most noble self.

NSC operates at interwoven governance levels—from grassroots communities through counties and regions to national levels. Its foundational principle: offer aid based solely on equity, justice, and progress tenets, enabling those in adversity to rise and unlock potential.

Every New-Way nation boasts robust NSC networks serving as compassionate governance backbones. These institutions offer diverse opportunities for contributing talents, resources, and energies toward greater good—through value donations, volunteering time and expertise, sharing knowledge, or advocating uplifting initiatives. Recipients and donors alike receive constructive feedback fostering self-awareness, trust, and purpose while lowering stress and increasing morale. This mechanism ensures efficient resource allocation while instilling profound fulfillment, recognizing that in giving and receiving, all are enriched materially and spiritually.

The NSC model integrates deeply into New-Way Governance frameworks, ensuring philanthropy principles weave into society's structure. Once resources are distributed equitably, any surplus goes toward strategic priorities identified by the government, whether advancing research, strengthening education and healthcare, building infrastructure, or enhancing social services that tackle each community's unique challenges.

Namibia, New Zealand, Slovenia, Sri Lanka, UAE, and Uruguay embraced NSC structure, recognizing its transformative power. New-Way policies align philanthropic activities with the LifeScore system while robust safeguards prevent resource abuse, ensuring benefits distributed fairly and ethically.

The comprehensive framework outlines donors' and recipients' rights and responsibilities. NSC tracks aid recipients' progress, ensuring genuine life improvement beyond material terms. However, no individual receives indefinite aid—once sufficiently empowered, recipients must transition from "needy" status, as able-bodied individuals are expected to contribute through their own efforts.

NSC welcomes contributions of every kind, material or spiritual. Anyone who assists the elderly with daily chores earns LifeScores while developing a sense of purpose and empathy. Schoolchildren are particularly encouraged in these activities. Able-bodied individuals offer labor for construction and maintenance projects. Every contribution is meticulously accounted for and allocated according to societal priorities. At this system's heart lies profound truth: fulfillment comes not from wealth accumulation but from giving and sharing. In extending helping hands, we uplift others materially while enriching ourselves spiritually.

The NSC model testifies to the power of collaboration—diverse voices united in vision where kindness and generosity aren't mere ideals but living realities permeating society.

In life's larger context, diversity isn't just a thread—it's the essence giving vibrancy and resilience. Vish captured this truth: "*Life flourishes in diversity but perishes in exclusivity.*"

These words resonated deeply with Kirl, whose commitment to New-Way Ideology left an indelible mark all around. Whether creating Sanctuary centers, setting up planetariums and NSC organizations, or delivering lectures, Kirl embodied this dictum, ensuring equal opportunity, dignity, and respect aligned with humanity's well-being.

Before the 22nd century, societies fell victim to a dangerous myopia, valuing technological achievements above all else while dismissing diversity as a mere annoyance. This narrow worldview marginalized Indigenous and weak communities and threatened planetary sustainability—a grave error that Vish sought to rectify by embracing the Prime Directive principle from Star Trek. Vish's vision was clear: "*No culture to be vaulted for storage.*" True progress cannot be achieved by preserving cultures as relics but by embracing and celebrating human diversity's rich tapestry in all vibrant hues.

Kirl echoed: "New-Way Ideologies facilitate socio-cultural equilibrium." The Core Team embraced these central tenets with unwavering conviction. Dignity and respect weren't platitudes but fundamental principles undergirding employment, resource access, and human interaction. Justice System branches were established and dedicated to upholding diversity and inclusiveness ideals at all governance levels.

However, the path to equity faced challenges from deep-rooted biases—class, caste, color, region, race, national and sexual orientations ingrained over generations. Vish understood this complexity: "*Humans flirt with inhumane actions. That ironically makes them human.*"

Viswas offered a solution: "LifeScore assignment is one big practical solution." The revolutionary metric quantifying positive societal impact rewards beneficial behaviors while discouraging actions undermining unity in diversity. By aligning LifeScore with core values, powerful incentive structures encourage embracing shared humanity and celebrating differences. This comprehensive approach recognizes existence's interconnectedness—true progress requires every voice heard, perspective valued, individual treated with dignity.

At the heart of this endeavor was: diversity isn't a threat but wellspring of strength. In the 22nd century's globalized society, navigating diverse perspectives isn't virtue but necessity—a survival skill determining collective ability to tackle complex challenges ahead. This urgency fuels Core Team efforts. They understand pursuing diversity isn't a fleeting trend but constant imperative shaping human civilization's trajectory.

Through Sanctuary centers celebrating local biome tapestries, planetariums inviting cosmic diversity contemplation, or thought-provoking discourses challenging preconceptions, the Core Team's work testifies to embracing diversity's transformative power.

***

The Continuum

Transcendence

In a quiet valley, Vish lay on a simple bed, his eyes closed, yet his mind wide awake. As the dying rays of sunset cast an ethereal glow across the quiet valley, Vish lay motionless. People across Earth and the space colonies turned their rapt attention to this remote place, though its exact location stayed a fiercely guarded secret. They solemnly witnessed the scene through holostream holo-casted widely on public and private networks. For Vish, immobile as he was, this was the sole exchange medium—the holostream. This was the setting of profound transition—the 50+ year old sage voice that had catalyzed humanity's awakening that might soon fall silent.

Within the valley's embrace lay simple anonymous dwelling, unadorned except for life-sustaining apparatus surrounding the near-still life form at its center. White bio-lattice tendrils twined across Vish's withered body, suffusing his cells with coded regenerative sequences. Iridescent tubules pulsed in sync with his labored breathing, oxygenating his blood and nourishing his organs to support that fragile spark of life. Vish was not old, but decades of relentless physical and mental efforts had taken a heavy toll on his health. Though his body had succumbed to the ravages of time, Vish's mind remained brilliantly lucid. He had mastered his mind to transcend physical pain.

His eyes fluttered open, for fleeting moments, taking in the loved ones gathered in silent vigil at his bedside.

Summoning his flailing strength, Vish managed fidgety but reassuring smiles. His weak but pointed gaze settled on Hya, whose naturally youthful features belied his true age in this era of genetic rejuvenation therapies. Vish's ardent admirer met his stare with tremulous pride. Kaleidoscopes of thought-images from Vish cascaded across the holoscreen. Each luminous fragment carried insights that welled up from transcendental depths—visions born from his tireless work to awaken humanity's collective consciousness.

"The turmoil you foresaw is indeed convulsing the great nation-states," Hya's mental voice echoed in the reverent chamber. "The old orders are crumbling in the fires of revolution you sowed as people cast off the self-destructive dogmas of the past."

Vish could read Hya's holostream conveying scenes of impassioned masses that thronged the public squares in the capitals, their paths of protest like unified rivers breaching the dams of authoritarianism. Images of brutalized civilians gave way to those of military units siding with the people, laying down their arms in refusal to perpetuate further violence and injustice. Concrete monoliths of power toppled before irresistible human spirits of freedom and dignity.

"In the searing fires of this turbulent upheaval, the New-Way Ideology was firmly establishing itself," Hya continued, his voice thick with passionate conviction that transpired on holostream for Vish to read. "Its core principles of universal human rights, ethical governance, and sustainable custodianship have pierced through the heavy, oppressive clouds that have long shrouded us. This ideology is not merely guiding light; it is the hospice nurturing and guiding our people toward the world you have always envisioned for us."

Hya's thought streams segued into vivid images of hastily assembled representative councils from across the planet, composed of people from all walks of life. These councils worked tirelessly to forge new governance frameworks, each dedicated to serving the greatest good for both humanity and the biosphere. Laws and policies once twisted to benefit the few were being rewritten to enshrine justice in equality, empowerment, and environmental stewardship as inviolable freedoms for all.

As Hya's torrent of insights ebbed, Nya picked up the psychic thread. Nya, another staunch supporter of Vish, representing the next generation, her radiant persona resonated with bright hope of humanity's new era.

"The outer colony worlds too are experiencing their own upheavals," she continued. "But these are temporary labor pains as our celestial diaspora struggles to be born anew under New-Way's luminous embrace."

Nya's thought stream conveyed bittersweet contrasts as blood-dimmed tides of civic violence gradually crested and receded, leaving in their wake the first glimmers of new cooperative and convivial eras even among off-world settlements.

As news of New-Way's ascendance spreads outward into space at unprecedented speeds," Nya intoned, "its ethos will help heal the deep divisions within our colonial diasporas. They will emerge from their crucibles as beacons of that higher vision—custodians, not conquerors, taking responsible stewardship of their new homes just as we are finally doing on our earthen Mother World."

Just then, the key member of the intimate family stepped forward, her timeless persona radiating clear, otherworldly light. Ani gently placed a hand on Vish's forehead, and serene calm washed over his face. Deep psychic connection formed between them as their minds briefly intertwined, surpassing the limits of the physical world.

In that blissful moment, Vish experienced what felt like final epiphany. His life's accumulated wisdom burst into vivid, cosmic understanding. The boundary between realities dissolved as his consciousness reached the ultimate frontier, glimpsing for an instant the profound truth behind all existence, all for one and one for all.

And in that epitome of realization, Vish clearly understood—this was not an ending, but a new beginning more wondrous than he could ever conceive. His mortal vehicle might have run its course, but now he would unleash the boundless potential of his consciousness from its bodily shackles. His role in catalyzing humanity's metamorphosis had reached its culmination. At last, his true eternal journey could commence—a quest of spiritual exploration and reunification with the ineffable source that gave rise to the cosmos—into the Elements.

As Ani withdrew her hand, the transcendent reverie dissipated, and Vish's eyes fluttered open once more, perhaps for the last time. His gaze swept over his assembled devotees, their faces awash in bittersweet joy and longing. Without a single word being uttered, they understood the heart song welling up within his consciousness. He was blissfully at peace, knowing that his mantle was being carried forward by devoted followers in perfect harmony.

Kaleidoscopes of memories celebrating his life shimmered through their shared consciousness. They saw his early days as an inspiring youth in an oppressed part of the world, his rise as a global voice uplifting humanity's potential, and the hard-fought struggles leading to the birth of New-Way civilization and beyond.

In his lucid moments, Vish allowed himself to truly feel the impact of his work, the radiant ethos he had helped foster, and the countless lives he had enriched and empowered. His was a legacy not of wealth or empire, but of upliftment and unconditional compassion that had transformed the destiny of the human species and its terrestrial homeland along with outer worlds.

As the labored breathing of his mortal body seemed stilled, a profound sense of grace and transition settled over the sanctum. Ani offered her thoughts as words echoing across the old and new worlds: "Our dearest friend, your mortal journey may have slowed, but you faced the injustices and brutalities of the old world with an incandescent vision—one that illuminated the path to human renewal and transcendence. Your wellspring of empathy, ethics, and custodial reverence for all life has cleansed the cesspool of our self-destructive past, allowing our people to reclaim their birthright as nature's dearest children. Your transcendence marks not an ending, but a new, boundless beginning—for you and for the human continuum you helped realize."

As Ani's voice dissipated across planetary and celestial audiences, Vish's bodily vessel shuddered before what seemed like falling into eternal sleep.

*****

About the Author

Viswa is the pen name of Mr. Durga N. Yalamanchi, a native of the Telugu-speaking state of Telangana, India. He holds master's degrees in English Literature and Business Administration, along with a Diploma in Computer Science, reflecting his diverse academic and intellectual pursuits.

Deeply influenced by his father's unwavering commitment to progressive ideals, Viswa draws inspiration from a wide array of thinkers and writers. Among them are renowned Telugu language authors such as "Sri Sri" and Vaddera Chandi Das, philosophical minds like Jiddu Krishnamurti, and towering figures of English literature such as John Milton, Samuel Johnson, William Shakespeare, Virginia Woolf, and William Faulkner.

Recognizing the need to reimagine the society through four interconnected primal constructs—judicial, political, economic, and social structures—all unified by spirituality, Viswa turned to storytelling. Through a stream-of-consciousness narrative, he aimed to deliver a direct message that resonated with the hearts and minds of people everywhere.

Made in United States
Cleveland, OH
05 November 2026

47645295R00122